The Odyssey of an Apple Thief

Judaic Traditions in Literature, Music, and Art
Harold Bloom and Ken Frieden, *Series Editors*

Select Titles in Judaic Traditions in Literature, Music, and Art

Benjamin Fondane's "Ulysses," Bilingual Edition
Nathaniel Rudavsky-Brody, trans.

*The Implacable Urge to Defame: Cartoon Jews
in the American Press, 1877–1935*
Matthew Baigell

Paul Celan: The Romanian Dimension
Petre Solomon; Emanuela Tegla, trans.

Petty Business
Yirmi Pinkus; Evan Fallenberg and Yardenne Greenspan, trans.

The People of Godlbozhits
Leyb Rashkin; Jordan Finkin, trans.

Pioneers: The First Breach
S. An-sky; Rose Waldman, trans.

Red Shoes for Rachel: Three Novellas
Boris Sandler; Barnett Zumoff, trans.

Vilna My Vilna: Stories by Abraham Karpinowitz
Helen Mintz, trans.

For a full list of titles in this series, visit
https://press.syr.edu/supressbook-series
/judaic-traditions-in-literature-music-and-art/.

The Odyssey of an Apple Thief

Moishe Rozenbaumas

Translated from the French by
Jonathan Layton

Edited by
Isabelle Rozenbaumas

With a Foreword by
Samuel Kassow

Syracuse University Press

Originally written in Yiddish, this book was first published in French as *L'odyssée d'un voleur de pommes* (Paris: La Cause des Livres, 2004).

All photographs are courtesy of Isabelle Rozenbaumas.

First Edition 2019

19 20 21 22 23 24   6 5 4 3 2 1

∞ The paper used in this publication meets the minimum requirements of the American National Standard for Information Sciences—Permanence of Paper for Printed Library Materials, ANSI Z39.48-1992.

For a listing of books published and distributed by Syracuse University Press, visit https://press.syr.edu.

ISBN: 978-0-8156-3626-7 (hardcover)
        978-0-8156-3644-1 (paperback)
        978-0-8156-5472-8 (e-book)

Library of Congress Control Number: 2019946990

Manufactured in the United States of America

I want to dedicate this book to my mother, Mere-Khaye, shot at the age of forty-five by the German murderers and their Lithuanian collaborators on the seventh of Elul 5701 (August 30–31, 1941) in Telz, Lithuania; to my brother Yosef, shot at the age of twenty-one on the twenty-first of Av[*] 1941 by the same murderers; to my brother Leybe, shot at the age of sixteen on the twenty-first of Av 1941 in Telz; and to my brother Eliahu, shot at age ten in the month of Av 1941 in Telz.

May they rest in peace.

I beseech my children, my grandchildren, and my great-grandchildren to never forget.

Moishe Rozenbaumas

[*] Another family source says the twenty-first of Tamouz (July 15–16, 1941), one month earlier, when the main massacre of Jewish men took place. The local Lithuanian perpetrators carried out several rounds of mass killings.

Contents

Illustrations

ix

Maps

Foreword

SAMUEL KASSOW

Moishe Rozenbaumas's *Odyssey of an Apple Thief* is a fascinating autobiography written in Yiddish by a resourceful and tough Lithuanian Jew. Rozenbaumas describes small-town Jewish life in interwar Lithuania, his wartime combat in a remarkable and little-known combat unit of the Red Army, family and work in postwar Vilnius, the risky decision to leave the Soviet Union, and finally a new life in France.

The Odyssey of an Apple Thief gives the English-language reader a rare glimpse into the rich and now vanished world of Lithuanian Jewry. Between the wars, Lithuanian Jewry numbered 154,000, or 7 percent of the population of interwar Lithuania, excluding the number the Jews from Vilna that belonged to Poland in this period. Compared to 3.5 million Polish Jewish or the 2 million Soviet Jews in this period, the Lithuanian Jewish community was quite small. But it developed an intense cultural life marked by a very strong Jewish identity. While Yiddish had begun to decline in the Soviet Union and even in Poland, practically all Lithuanian Jews continued to speak Yiddish as their first language, and very many had a good knowledge of Hebrew. Almost 90 percent of Jewish children attended Jewish schools—religious, Zionist, and secular democratic—the highest percentage in Europe. Nowhere else in the diaspora were Jews as "comfortable in their own skin," as unself-consciously and proudly Jewish, as they were in Lithuania.

Rozenbaumas spent most of his youth in the town of Telsiai (Telz in Yiddish). It was a beautiful town, nestled along the shores of Lake

Mastis. Jews had settled there as early as the fifteenth century, and for much of the nineteenth century it had a Jewish majority. In 1923, one year after Rozenbaumas was born, there were 1,545 Jews out of a total population of 4,691.

In Jewish lore and in Jewish memory, Telz is known and celebrated for its traditions of piety and learning and for the great rabbis—Eliezer Gordon, Yosef Leyb Bloch, and others—who upheld the high cultural standards of Lithuanian Jewry. Its main claim to fame was its celebrated yeshiva, which attracted avid Talmud students from all over the world. (After the Holocaust it was reconstituted in Cleveland, Ohio.)

Jewish Telz had ample reason to boast of its exalted traditions. Especially because the entire community was brutally murdered in 1941, there was an understandable tendency in the memorial literature to err on the side of hagiography. This Rozenbaumas does not do. He shows Jewish life through a different lens: the desperate struggles of impoverished Jews living in grim hovels, the class tensions in the town, left-wing radical politics that was a world apart from the renowned yeshiva or the superb Hebrew education that many middle-class Jews gave their children, in particular their daughters. While many memories of Jewish life in Eastern Europe focus on close-knit and loving families that bravely survived good times and bad, here too Rozenbaumas tells a somewhat different story. His mother was, to be sure, loving and heroic. But his father, in effect, deserted his family during the depths of the Great Depression, fled to France, and left his penniless family in a desperate situation. All the more striking, therefore, is Rozenbaumas's painfully honest account of the fraught reunion with that same father many years after the end of the war.

Rozenbaumas does not paint a negative and harrowing picture of Lithuanian Jewish relations before World War II. Lithuanians and Jews were not particularly close, but they lived side by side, just as they had for generations. While popular and economic anti-Semitism exerted growing pressure on Lithuanian Jewry, especially in the late

1930s, Jews there suffered from far less anti-Semitic violence than in neighboring Poland or Romania. Jewish schools received state support. When Germany invaded Poland in September 1939, fifteen thousand Polish Jews found refuge in Lithuania, and by and large they were treated decently by the Lithuanian government.

If any reasonable person had judged Lithuanian-Jewish relations based on the reality of 1939, he would have been at a loss to explain the massive upsurge of Lithuanian anti-Semitism and the resulting large-scale collaboration of Lithuanian society in the mass murder of Jews in the second half of 1941. A key explanation is the disastrous effect of the Soviet occupation of Lithuania on Lithuanian-Jewish relations.

In June 1940, the Soviet Union suddenly took over the Baltic republics. As a brutal wave of repression crushed Lithuanian independence, resentful Lithuanians looked to Nazi Germany as the one power that might deliver them from hated Kremlin rule. Their Jewish neighbors naturally preferred Soviet to Nazi rule, just as, to paraphrase one Jewish leader, one naturally prefers life imprisonment to a death sentence.

Soon large sections of Lithuanian society became convinced that Lithuanian Jewry had betrayed their country through massive collaboration with the Soviets. Jews supposedly controlled the government and the police. It was Jews, it was widely believed, who hustled their Lithuanian neighbors onto trains bound for Siberia.

The truth was more complex. The leaders of the government and the police were not Jewish. Jews made up a large proportion of those individuals deported to Siberia, larger than their share of the overall population. Soviet nationalization of small business and private trade wiped out the Jewish middle class. Communist repression crushed religious life and Zionist political activity.

On the other hand, poorer Jews did receive opportunities for social advancement and employment that they did not have in independent Lithuania. *The Odyssey of an Apple Thief* offers some revealing insights into this turbulent period. Rozenbaumas seems to have shed few tears for the loss of Lithuanian independence, and he himself seems to have supported what he then believed to be the establishment of a more just and equal society.

When Germany invaded the Soviet Union, Rozenbaumas was one of the small minority of Lithuanian Jews—perhaps fifteen thousand—who managed to outrun the panzer divisions and escape to the interior of the USSR. There, after many hardships that included a stint of slave labor on an Uzbek collective farm, he joined the Red Army and served in its 16th Lithuanian Division.

No fighting unit in World War II, with the exception of the Jewish Brigade of the British army, had a larger proportion of Jews than the 16th Lithuanian Division. Most Lithuanians, to put it mildly, did not support the Soviet cause. So although political expediency dictated the formation of a division that was called "Lithuanian," a large percentage of its soldiers, especially in its early days, were Jewish. In some platoons, orders were actually given in Yiddish. The division suffered terrible casualties. In its baptism of fire, at Alekseyevka near Orel in 1943, Soviet commanders ordered the division to make a suicidal frontal attack on German positions. The attack turned into a bloody fiasco. But as Jewish soldiers, whose numbers were steadily whittled away, learned of massacre of their families back home, they fought with exemplary courage. Four Jewish soldiers of the division received the USSR's highest medal for bravery, Hero of the Soviet Union. Of the five thousand Jewish soldiers who fought in the division, two thousand were killed in action. A survey of survivors who emigrated to Israel revealed that 75 percent were wounded at least once and 40 percent at least twice. Rozenbaumas himself, who was wounded multiple times, served in a reconnaissance unit of the division whose members were overwhelmingly non-Jewish. These memoirs give the English-language reader invaluable insight into the everyday reality of combat in the Red Army.

With the war over, Rozenbaumas started a new life in Vilnius. He married, began a family, and, thanks to his war record and his membership in the Communist Party, became the associate director of a vocational school. Rozenbaumas gives a fascinating and revealing account of how the Soviet economy really worked on the local level: the pervasive graft, diversion of supplies, the falsification of records. Quite aware that a position of power always carried with it the danger of arrest, Rozenbaumas decided to return to his prewar profession, tailoring and clothes styling. In his last years in Vilnius, his skill at internecine infighting and his understanding of the communist bureaucracy gave him and his family a very comfortable life by Soviet standards. But in the face of Soviet anti-Semitism, Rozenbaumas began to feel growing doubts about the Soviet system and began to listen to the pleas of his wife, Reyzele, to try to leave the Soviet Union. Vilnius Jews who could prove prior Polish citizenship had a narrow window to leave the USSR in 1956–57. While Rozenbaumas's wife, Reyzele, was made a Polish citizen through forged papers, Rozenbaumas was not. Only a very hefty and very risky bribe could procure the false documents that enabled the family to finally leave the USSR.

The account of the family's journey to France, of the fraught and tense reunion with Rozenbaumas's father, of his successful struggle to start a business and achieve some measure of security and independence for his wife and two children is a fascinating story in itself and a fitting coda to *The Odyssey of an Apple Thief*. It is a testament to human perseverance.

Preface and Acknowledgments

Moishe Rozenbaumas

The idea of writing about my life and about my murdered family massacred by Germans and Lithuanians was tormenting me for a long time already.

Around the family table, when the family is together, we sometimes evoke the past with the children and grandchildren, but the meal's etiquette inevitably turns the attention either to the sequence of dishes or to current events and lends itself little to a consistent conversation. Besides, I'm not a particularly good storyteller, and I fear putting the spotlight on myself. It was therefore only by short anecdotal fragments that I was conveying the events of my life. In taking up the pen, I do want to pour out my heart but also provide a big-picture view of my life's unfolding, and I dare to hope that one day my children, grandchildren, and children of our grandchildren will take an interest in this account. I am writing for them.

Where to begin such an endeavor? At seventy years old, memory begins to show signs of weakness, and if you can no longer well remember where you put your glasses, old memories sometimes return with surprising clarity. There are still, however, gaps and murky areas that one searches in vain to fill.

Before beginning to reel off these memories, I want to pay homage to the editors and authors who contributed to the Memorial

Book of my city of Telz, in the *Sefer Telz*,[1] and bow before the merits and extent of their work, a work of the preservation of memory first and foremost, as much as a work of history. Our generation will soon pass; its ranks are thinning, and this work will remain a bible for our children and the children of our children. One way or another, we who have survived must do all in our power to preserve this memory, in order to leave traces for the coming generations.

Now I would like to say a few words concerning the authors of the *Sefer Telz*, those who traveled this hard road and survived, as well as those who left the country before the war and were not present to witness the calamity that struck our people but who lost their kin who remained behind. Each of us has a singular take on things at each moment that is specific to his own existence. The same event will be perceived and understood in diverse ways by different protagonists. It's not insignificant whether you account for an event in the moment or forty or fifty years later. You don't look at the world with the same eyes at twenty years of age as you do when you are sixty or seventy. What we have preserved of it is not necessarily what the eyes have seen. It may well happen that when recalling a fact that happened a long time before, we are under the impression that we were there to see it, yet we may have simply heard it spoken about and have no knowledge of it other than through hearsay. By dint of telling and retelling the story of an episode, some end up believing they had been witnesses to it. What I'm saying here, of course, applies equally to me. Thus, each of us tells his story and the drama he has gone through as he has seen and heard them, but also as he has reconstructed them, even if he or she does not, or cannot, distinguish one from the other.

1. A number of *yizker bikher* are now available online on the website of the New York Public Library. The link to Yitzhak Alperovitz, ed., *Sefer Telz* (Tel Aviv: Telz Society, 1984), is https://digitalcollections.nypl.org/items/0031d440-3554-0133 -535c-00505686d14e.

My constant worry in writing has been not to offend anyone. I was born not in Telz but in Memel, in East Prussia, and my parents lived in Gorzd (Gargždai). However, from barely age six until eighteen, I spent the years of my youth in Telz in Lithuania; my family died there, with the exception of my father, as we shall see, and whether I want to or not, I consider myself more a Telzer than a Parisian. That said, I have made an effort to write what I saw with my eyes and heard with my ears. Not wishing to diminish my testimony or to hurt whomever it might be, because most of the major players in this story have long since left this world, I have made the decision not to use anyone's real name. If I have, however, without wishing to, offended someone, I here ask for their forgiveness.

If my perspective is distinct from that of the authors of the *Sefer Telz*, it is because my road has been different. Nevertheless, I feel infinitely close to them, and I know their suffering because it has been my own. When they recall their tragedies, I see my brothers and my mother. Lending a hand in assembling this remembrance is a sacred task, although the endeavor is not self-evident. To get hold of this remembrance, I had to dig deep down inside of myself. At times, I stopped writing, as if my hand was refusing its cooperation. I don't conceal that it was a question of mind and not the hand. I had to wait for this affliction to stop and for the desire to free my heart to return. Now I feel pressed to put a final period to this work. I write this account essentially so that my children and my grandchildren will not be ignorant of what our people have gone through during the twentieth century, what their parents and grandparents have experienced, because time flies by, because I am already seventy-two years old, because no one has signed a contract with God, and because, for all of us, our time is limited.

Paris, summer of 1994

Acknowledgments

First and foremost, God is the one to be thanked. If not for his protection, there would be no book.

To my friend Tuvie Bal-Shem, the world president of the survivors from Telz with whom I maintained a regular correspondence, I render deep homage.[2] I am thankful for the advice he gave me on the manuscript initially written in Yiddish. He was the first person whose opinion I sought, given his experience as a redactor and editor of the great *yizker bukh Sefer Telz*. He had been the backbone and the head of the endeavor I described in the beginning of this book. He had mainly liked my text because I pondered the social question of the impoverished of Telz. He was so taken by it that he began to read it aloud in front of the annual general assembly of the survivors and, without even asking me, began to look for a publisher in Hebrew and Yiddish. It was then too early to print it, I told him. Only much later did I embrace the idea. I respect him enormously and thank him for everything.

I am grateful to my daughter, Isabelle, for her help when it came to disentangling the difficult-to-read manuscript that I had translated from Yiddish to French—or, more precisely, into Judeo-French. Isabelle worked a lot with me, using her savoir faire in the field of writing, her experience in translation, and her style, with enough perceptiveness not to change the content of the text.

My Yiddish text, which I began in 1994 and finished in 1997, has waited for my daughter to finish her translations. I have read all of them with a wonder mingled with pleasure. When she finished one book, another translation was waiting for her. It is the reason I began to translate myself, but as I was not educated in France, there were of course a lot of errors. Finally, in 1999, she found the time for me. As you can see, small causes produce big effects. I wanted my daughter and no other translator to help me complete this work, knowing that she would surely understand me and, if not, that I would be able to explain to her in Yiddish.

---

2. Tuvie Bal-Shem passed away in 2011. He was one of the main and first informants in the editor's project about Jewish girls' education provided in the Telzer Gymnasium Yavne: Bat Kama At? See http://batkamaat.org/?attachment_id=1037.

Acknowledgments

ISABELLE ROZENBAUMAS

For Moishe's grandchildren, Eléonore, Emmanuel, Mélinée, and Vadim, and great-grandchildren, Aharon, David, Hadassa, Leila, Naomi, Rafael, Sarah, and Shmuel.

The urge to write his memoirs resulted in the first place from Moishe Rozenbaumas's acute awareness that the memory of the Jewish Ashkenazic world where he was born might well vanish and that the historical events he went through and was an actor of could be wiped from memory after him and therefore lost for future generations. He saw in his children, grandchildren, and great-grandchildren the first depositories of this legacy and conceived the knowledge of the historical reality he witnessed as a compass for them. What I owe to my father has a lot to do with his discernment and deep understanding of situations, human beings, and life. If not for that, I would not be here to convey the story.

Over the years, from the publication of the French edition, *L'odyssée d'un voleur de pommes* (Paris: La Cause des Livres, 2004), to the present English edition, many people have contributed to bringing these memoirs to the public.

The first one who recognized the power of Moishe's narrative was Martine Lévy, who had inaugurated her publishing house with the testimony of her own father, Jean-Claude Dreyfus, *Souvenirs lointains de Buchenwald et Dora.* She helped me to channel the obsessive fidelity of my translation within the realms required by French elegance. I am thankful for her support for each artistic project born from the book, her friendly presence, and her gracious enthusiasm.

My gratitude to my Yiddish teacher and close friend Yitskhok Niborski cannot fully be expressed, and not only for the preface he wrote to the French edition. Without all he imparted to me, his generous counsel on all of my translations from Yiddish, neither this translation nor any other project that I embraced would have been the same. This goes back to reading Kulbak's *Zelmenyaner* under his guidance, almost forty years ago, and reopening the doors of my family's Yiddish, Russian, and Soviet history. My outstanding teacher Rachel Ertel has helped me carve this sensitivity through the Yiddish poets in the context of the Russian modernity, all things in the background of this translation.

Over the years, friends who have given voice to Moishe, J. F. Fontayne, Charles Rappoport, Michel Grosman as well as Charles Goldszlagier for the French online Radio Yiddish pour Tous, or have staged artistic creations based on Moishe's Yiddish narrative, have allowed me to imagine the scenic potential of his life experience, a fascinating interplay of personal drama and history. My daughter Eléonore Biezunski's *La complainte du balluchon* (The Complaint of the Bundle) was a creative transposition—in Yiddish songs—of her grandfather's stories and adventures in the world of klezmer music. Artist and interpreter Laurent d'Aumale was always present in songs and friendship. Even as they worked on my project related to my mother, Rosa Portnoi, I feel it is fair to express my gratitude to Lithuanian artists Romualdas Inčirauskas and Zita Inčirauskienė and their students at Telšiai Art Academy and playwright Laimutė Pocevičienė and the pupils of her theatrical workshop in Telšiai. Painter and sculptor France Hilbert and recently Bart Bakker, who painted two amazing portraits of my parents, are witnesses to the spiritual effect of Moishe and Rosa on the world. My parents have been two trees growing entwined.

Second-time immigrant that I am, my confidence to undertake the journey with *The Odyssey of an Apple Thief* would not have been the same without the fabric of friendship woven by a spiritual and intellectual family that has surrounded me in the United States. Some of them are authors whom I have translated into French and whose work has influenced me, but all of them have enlightened me with their knowledge and wit. Jonathan Boyarin, my Telzer landsman who followed me to Cleveland, where I interviewed the Rebbetsins from the Bloch family (to which he is related), and Elissa Sampson, Nahma Sandrow, and William Meyers; Robert Alter and Carol Cosman (who translated one of my presentations into English); and David Biale and his wife, Rachel Biale, who holds a fascinating document from her mother, Anina Korati, *A Diary: December 10, 1939–April 16, 1942*; Vicki Brower and Michael Gottesman; France Hilbert; Emily Socolov and Itzik Gottesman; Suzan Leon; and Janet Leuchter are among these loyal friends who supported me in my American exploration of culture.

Since I moved to this country, my dear professor and friend the historian Pierre Vidal-Naquet (1930–2006) has passed away. With humor and fondness, he used to suggest—against evidence—that my father, a compulsive reader, must have read Augustine's episode about his theft of pears (*Confessions*, bk. 2, ll. 9–14). I had to find myself mentors in my new country. Through their books, seminars, and public expression, as well as in conversation, Barbara Kirshenblatt-Gimblett and Samuel Kassow played this role for me. Not only did they support my research and projects, but they also offered many paths to deepen my approach to Jewish history and culture in Eastern Europe, a precious guideline on which I relied to work on my father's book. Robert Shapiro has offered useful insights and conversations on religious thought and social life since we met in Jerusalem decades ago.

Jonathan Brent, the executive director of YIVO, was a challenging adviser, open to dialogue on all the issues raised by the history of the Jews under communism. His seminars nurtured my old-time fascination for Bulgakov, Isaac Babel, and Vasili Grosman. From the time that I translated the book from Yiddish to French until the present preparation of the English edition, I benefited from books, conversations, seminars, lectures, and insights from a number of scholars and Yiddish connoisseurs who have enriched my understanding. I am grateful for the wealth of information and reflection they brought to my attention: Michael Alpert, Saulius Beržinis, Nikolai Borodulin, Dovid Braun, Emil Dreitser (author of *Shush! Growing Up Jewish under Stalin*), Gennady Estraykh, Yevgeniy Fiks, David E. Fishman (with his enlightening *Book Smugglers*), Paul Hershl Glasser, Grant Gochin, Itzik Gottesman, Saul Issroff, Rokhl Kafrissen, Sergey Kanovitch, Samuel Kassow, Barbara Kirshenblatt-Gimblett, Lara Lempert, Suzanne Leon, David Mazower, Martin Miller, Naomi Seidman, Amanda Miryem-Khaye Seigel, Robert Shapiro, Yelena Shmulenson, Lyudmila Sholokhova, Zisl Slepovitch, Shaul Stampfer, Saulius Sužiedėlis, Paula Teitelbaum, Steve Zipperstein, and Efraim Zuroff. Carole Lemée, an anthropologist who works on the crimes committed against the Jewish population of Lithuania, has traveled the country from one massacre place to another, not forgetting to place candles for Rosa and Moishe in Telz.

This book would not have been published without the friendly advice of Itsik Gottesman to present the English manuscript to Ken Frieden, who immediately manifested interest for the initial version of the translation and encouraged me to submit the project to Syracuse University Press. The present version was first edited by Eric Heuberger and again revised by myself and the translator, Jonathan Layton. I am deeply thankful to both of them. Jonathan has probably won his place in the world to come: sitting at my side, patiently going through each word and turn of phrase, diving into the most minuscule semantic nuance that I wanted to be sure to convey fully in English. We mutually benefited in our master class in translation. Amélie Ducroux, from the University Lyon 2, in France, has helped me efficiently locate the passages of the authors that my father quotes in the last chapter in their English editions. Dovid Braun has offered his amazing expertise in dialectology and phonetics.

I owe to Yeva Lapsker a new translation of Franz Kafka's fragment (*Das nächste Dorf*, 1919) that made it obvious why I chose this epigraph in the first place. Working with geographer and cartographer Jacques Enaudeau, who provided three original maps, was a

pleasure and a grace, no less than having my daughter Eléonore Biezunski work with my father on the map of the original French book.

I cannot thank enough Deborah Manion, acquisitions editor at
Syracuse University Press, for her kindness, patience, attention, and
great professionalism in the support she offered to me. All the team
was very helpful at each step of the work. I was lucky that the English version was placed in Annette Wenda's hands for copy editing. I
could not have wished for a more respectful and sensitive approach
to the text.

It is fair to come back now to my father and my family. My husband, Michel Biezunski, provided much more than the technological
support needed to navigate the digital world, his department; he also
maintained with his legendary sense of humor and fondness the conditions so that I could accomplish this labor of love while he protects
me as much as he can from the outside material world. Love is not a
rare commodity in our family. Nobody valued more my emotional
and practical investment in this work than my brother, Alexandre
(Sacha) Rozenbaumas, and Micheline, my sister-in-law. During all
these years, they never got tired of my narrative of the narrative, of
my permanent commentary on the text. They are the pillars of my
life now that our parents are gone. In the realm of brotherhood,
my cousin Cyril who accompanied me in Lithuania—with the Meyerowitz ancestors and tribe in our heart—was at my side since I was
a rebellious teenager. The broader family played a part they cannot
imagine and supported me tirelessly: Laurent d'Aumale, Nadia Broit-
man, my late friend Francine Burgerman and her son Thomas, Jac-
queline Carnaud, Michel Grosman, France Hilbert, Salomeja Josade
and her sister Elżbieta, Alain Le Roy, Yitskhok and Estela Niborski, Catherine Skoda-Schmoll and her daughter Lia Schmoll, my late
friend Thierry Schmoll, Daniele Weiler, and Olivia Zarcate.

Moishe had an acute sense of psychology, an aspect of his deep
understanding of the world. He was able to grasp in a very deep
way the personality of each one of his grandchildren. My daughters,
Mélinée and Eléonore, who are as loving and supportive as children
can be, as well as my brother's sons, Emmanuel and Vadim, have

embraced Moishe's legacy each in her or his own way. It is fair to shed light on Eléonore's artistic creativity, bringing to life and at the center of her life a legacy deeply rooted in my parents' Yiddish culture and Jewish history. It's for all of them and for their children that Moishe wrote, because he knew that his testimony, based on what he had seen and heard, would be like a lighthouse for them.

Note on Languages, Translations, and Mapping

Isabelle Rozenbaumas

Moishe Rozenbaumas passed away on November 1, 2016. At the time, Jonathan Layton had already translated the French book, and we had begun to entertain the idea of an English edition.

Languages

Not unlike Moishe himself, *The Odyssey of an Apple Thief* traveled a long way, going back and forth many times, first from Yiddish to French, now from French to English, always leaning soundly on the original Yiddish manuscript and, for this version, on Moishe's own Yiddish-language recording of his manuscript. During the translation process, the French translator, now the editor of this English version, was always accompanied by the author: in person while she established the French version, published by La Cause des Livres in 2004, he was literally sitting at her side and by recordings of his voice, which she listened to while revising the version now being published by Syracuse University Press, worried that anything added in the French version might be omitted.

While Moishe's narrative bristles with Yiddish names, Yiddish and Hebrew concepts, and Russian vocabulary, we are surprised not to find almost a single Lithuanian word. This fact in itself speaks to the invisible barrier separating the Jewish working youth from the ethnic Lithuanian population. The Jews had "only" been in the country for the past seven hundred years. Moishe's grandparents on his mother's side lived in Gorzd (Gargždai), one of the oldest Jewish communities, attested in the archival sources as far back as the sixteenth century.[1] Multilingualism was a hallmark of Jewish life in this corner of Lithuania. The author's mother, Mere-Khaye, a simple woman, could read and speak German, speak Lithuanian with her neighbors, used Yiddish as her vernacular and could probably read and write it, and prayed in Hebrew. From this shtetl, which Sholem Aleichem might have described as being as "large as a yawn," the United States Holocaust Memorial Museum in Washington, DC, owns a photo with the caption "Group portrait of an Esperanto class in Gargždai, Lithuania," dated 1940.[2]

Instead of one final glossary accounting for this polyglossia, it made more sense to import this multilingual corpus into the text itself, translating in apposition, polishing it, paraphrasing, and adding a footnote only when a notion needs more context, because this juxtaposition was in the logic of the author's writing itself and embedded in his oral culture. This very method of commenting on words from different languages had also been part of the process of elaboration of the French version when my father and I sat together trying to figure out how to match his original Yiddish text, my understanding of it, and his own French translation in what I have called *tate-loshn*, a mirror expression to *mame-loshn*, the mother

1. See Nancy Schoenburg and Stuart Schoenburg, *Lithuanian Jewish Communities* (Northvale, NJ: Jason Aronson, 1996), 104: "Gorzhd is near Memel (9 miles) on the German border. It had one of the first Jewish communities in Lithuania. In the cemetery there were tombstones over 400 years old. Documents from the sixteenth century mention Jews from Gorzhd as overseers for the collection of customs fees at the border. In 1639, they received a letter granting them full citizenship rights from Wladislaw IV, King of Poland. In 1742, King August III reissued this document."

2. Photograph no. 21860, courtesy of George Birman: https://collections.ushmm.org/search/catalog/pa1079425.

language. His answers to my questions contributed by amending and enriching the narrative. Indeed, each leg on this journey has been a very Jewish mode of expanding a text by adding levels of exegesis and commentaries.

Names, Romanization, and Pronunciation of Yiddish

For reasons he explains himself in his short preface, Moishe has preferred not to name most of the persons he is remembering, tinting his narrative with a more collective quality and conferring on his testimony a historical or sometimes sociological character. The Yiddish names of the members of our family are rendered in the Yiddish inflection they were pronounced with and written by my parents and more precisely the way my father has transcribed them in his French autotranslation and in the forms he conveyed to Yad Vashem. In general, but even more for Moishe's first name, I tried to maintain coherence between the French and the English translations, so as to avoid the same Yiddish name having a different romanization in each language.

For most Yiddish words, I have adopted the standard YIVO transliteration chart, as in *khasene* (marriage), *khokhme* (wit), and *kneydlekh*. I refrained from adding footnotes of this sort: "*kneydlekh*: matzo balls." Names of prayers are generally mentioned in their Hebrew—and not Yiddish—pronunciation.

It was suggested to me to transcribe names and words according to their pronunciation in the Lithuanian Yiddish dialect, which covers a geographical zone much larger than the borders of present-day Lithuania (see map 1), including parts of (northern) Belorussia as well as Russia. Over the years, I noticed that Yiddish-speaking families sometimes reproduce characteristics of their vernacular from a town or from a religious background, such as Hasidic, where the *loshn-kodesh*, the Hebrew component of Yiddish, can expand so much as to become opaque to a secular speaker. The Yiddish may present *daytshmerism* (Germanization), revealing a more intellectual or assimilated Jewish milieu. The Yiddish language is more or less tinted with and influenced by the language of the country. Moishe, whose father's family was from Warsaw, had a distinctive—not to say idiosyncratic—difficulty in differentiating the sounds *s* from *z*, *sh* or the *g/j*, possibly characteristic of Lithuanian Yiddish. His wife, Rosa, born and raised in Samogitia (Žemaitija), the western region of Lithuania, had a less obvious Lithuanian Yiddish. On the tapes recorded by Moishe, I was able to perceive some very fine distinctions I never noticed before in conversation, like the sound of the French word *oeil* [œj] and not "ey" [ej], as often heard, for "oy" in words such as *broyt* (bread), *aroys* (out), and *farkoyfn* (to sell), which appears to be a feature of this region's Yiddish.[3] Regional differences inside Lithuania must have been very subtle, and almost imperceptible except to linguists. While striking to a native speaker of Polish or Ukrainian Yiddish as different from his own vernacular, it needs a trained ear to distinguish Litvish from standard Yiddish. To translate phonetically these minuscule inflections would require a strong literary or ethnographic goal. Therefore, it is preferable to stick to standard Yiddish and to give access to Moishe's recordings in his consistent Litvish Yiddish of the whole initial manuscript to anyone interested in dialectology. The original cassettes and their digitized copy are available for consultation at the YIVO Institute for Jewish Research.[4]

Mapping and Contextualizing

The map that was presented in the French edition was the result of the common work of Moishe with his granddaughter Eléonore Biezunski, then a student in geography. My father had drawn his

3. I am grateful to Dovid Braun, Yiddish linguist and teacher, who brought these small nuances to my attention. When I traveled in Lithuania in 2000, I was told by a survivor from Shavel (Šiauliai) that I spoke the Yiddish from Samogitia that he hadn't heard since long before, which I was not aware of.

4. YIVO Institute for Jewish Research: https://www.yivo.org/sound.

itinerary through Europe and Asia with his pattern-designer needle-point tracer on the map she had prepared for him. The task of remapping the odyssey of Moishe finally fell on geographer and cartographer Jacques Enaudeau, who provides three maps: "Lithuania on the eve of World War II," which presents the names of the towns and cities in their Yiddish transliteration as well as in the language of their then national space; "The journey of Moishe Rozenbaumas"; and "War and Holocaust on the Eastern Front." A number of historical notes have been added that didn't seem necessary almost twenty years ago because the readers might have been more familiar with certain aspects of history at that time.

As stated in Yitskhok Niborski's preface to the French edition, the original text was written by Moishe in a beautiful Yiddish. This book is also a tool to understand the Yiddish culture and history of this "Ruined Garden."[5] All in all, the choices that have been made here propose a path to enter into Moishe's cultural world in a vivid way, allowing the reader to sense the Jewish atmosphere of the interwar era, in this specific place that was Lithuania, but also to measure the weight of history on the Jewish society through the eyes of an individual with exceptional gifts of observation and analyses in conditions of hardship.

5. Jonathan Boyarin and Jack Kugelmass, eds. and trans., *From a Ruined Garden: The Memorial Books of Polish Jewry*, 2nd ed. (Bloomington: Indiana Univ. Press, 1998).

The Odyssey of an Apple Thief

"Unter dayne vayse shtern"

Unlike my siblings, I was born in the city of Memel (present-day Klaipeda) on the Baltic Sea on May 1, 1922.[1] My parents were then living in Gorzd (Gargždai in Lithuania),[2] which was where my mother had been born and where her family had lived for a long time. I never discovered how my father, Yitzkhak, came to be born in Vilna,[3] since Warsaw was where his parents lived and where he grew up. Taken prisoner by the Germans during the First World War and held captive in the Lithuanian shtetl of Gorzd, he remained there after the war and married my mother, Mere-Khaye (Mira). My brother Yosef was born there, three years ahead of me, my brother Leybe two years after me. Later, our brother Elie, whom my father would never know, was born of this marriage. Finally, my half-sister, Françoise, was born of my father's second marriage, in France, after the war.

My mother's father, Aaron Meyerowitz, was a big, strong man and must have been close to six and a half feet tall. He was a grain merchant with a booming voice that would overwhelm the peasants

---

"Unter dayne vayse shtern" is the title of a poem by Vilner poet Avrom Sutzkever that became a popular song: "Under Your White Stars."

1. Memel belonged to Germany until 1919. With the Treaty of Versailles it remained under the control of the Entente (principally France) and was returned to Lithuania in 1923.

2. Gargždai is one of the first Jewish settlements in Lithuania, in Yiddish Gorzd, גארזד. See https://www.jewishgen.org/yizkor/Gargzdai/gar413.html.

3. Presently known as Vilnius, capital of Lithuania.

in the marketplace who were afraid of triggering his rage and looked at him twice before raising their tone of voice when speaking to him. His wife, Tsivia (née Ackerman), was his opposite—a tiny woman with a voice that was calm and gentle. Her family was also from Gargždai. My mother had two sisters, Basye and Beyle, and a brother, Zushe. On my father's side of the family, I knew no one.

As I have said, my grandfather Aaron was in the grain-trading business. After the First World War, economic conditions in Lithuania were difficult, and many of the young people left in search of greener pastures. My mother's two sisters emigrated to America, got married, and started families. Her brother, Zushe, first traveled alone to South Africa, where a substantial community of Lithuanian Jews was already established, and then came back and took his family there. Already being the father of several children didn't prevent him from enlarging the family once he got to South Africa.

Lithuania is a small and beautiful country, flat and covered by innumerable forests, coursing with rivers and dotted by lakes. When I was a child, the population was essentially rural and peasant. Mechanization was still in the future, and labor was accomplished with the aid of draft horses. Large landholdings were the exception. The typical peasant owned a small plot of land along with a pair of horses and perhaps a few cows and raised some poultry, mostly chickens and geese, both for market and for consumption by his own family. Hog farming was fairly well developed but was primarily done for export.

The Jewish population was densely established in cities and towns. Jews represented a not so insignificant 10 percent of Lithuania's two and a half million people, but in certain towns composed half, if not more, of the population. They were businessmen, skilled tradesmen, artisans, cobblers, and tailors, and they held many other positions, notably in the professions. The majority were observant, particularly those who lived in towns of fewer than ten or fifteen thousand, the typical *shtetlekh*. As elsewhere, anti-Semitism was not a rare commodity; nevertheless, Jews had long-standing roots in the region, and Lithuanians worked and did business with them. Jewish

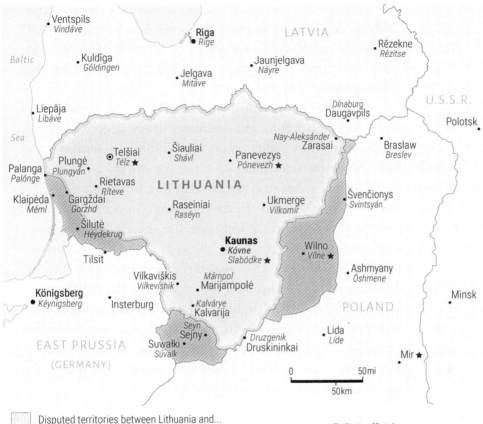

Baltic

Sea

Ventspils
Vindáve

Riga
Rîge

LATVIA

Kuldīga
Góldingen

Jaunjelgava
Náyre

Rēzekne
Rézitse

Jelgava
Mitáve

U.S.S.R.

Liepāja
Libáve

Dínaburg
Daugavpils

Polotsk

Palanga
Palónge

Plungė
Plungyán

Telšiai
Télz ★

Šiauliai
Shávl

Nay-Aleksánder
Zarasai

Braslaw
Breslev

Panevezys
Pónevezh ★

Rietavas
Ríteve

LITHUANIA

Švenčionys
Svintsyán

Klaipėda
Méml

Gargždai
Gorzhd

Raseiniai
Raséyn

Ukmerge
Vilkomír

Šilutė
Héydekrug

Kaunas
Kóvne
Slabódke ★

Wilno
Vílne ★

Ashmany
Óshmene

Tilsit

Vilkaviškis
Vilkevíshik

Márnpol
Marijampolė

Minsk

Königsberg
Kéynigsberg

Insterburg

Kalvárye
Kalvarija

POLAND

EAST PRUSSIA

Seyn
Sejny

Suwałki
Súvalk

Druzgenik
Druskininkai

Lida
Líde

(GERMANY)

Mir ★

0   50mi
|_____|
50km

◫ Disputed territories between Lithuania and...

Telšiai   official name
Télz   yiddish name (if different)

▩ Germany

   1920 separated from Germany as part of the Treaty of Versailles
   1920-23 administered by the French under a League of Nations mandate
   1924-38 annexed by Lithuania and granted autonomous status
   1939 turned over by Lithuania to Nazi Germany after an oral ultimatum

• capital city
◉ town where Moishe grew up
• other notable towns
★ important yeshivas

▩ Poland

   1918 claimed by independent Lithuania and Poland
   1920 recognized by the Soviet Union as part of Lithuania
   1920-22 annexed by Poland, leading Lithuania to break diplomatic ties

Sources: De Groot, Michael, *Building The New Order: 1938-1945*, The Spatial
History Project, 2010; Hiden, John and Lane, Thomas (eds.) *The Baltic and the
Outbreak of the Second World War*. Cambridge University Press, 1992; Katz,
Dovid, *Lîte. The Classic Litvak Territory*, 2015.

Cartography: Jacques Enaudeau, 2018

1. Lithuania on the eve of World War II. (Courtesy of Jacques Enaudeau.)

religious and cultural movements could be found everywhere, and they met with no restrictions from the independent government of Lithuania that was established just after the First World War and remained in power until the Soviet occupation, the result of the Molotov-Ribbentrop Pact of 1939.[4]

In the past, Lithuania was familiar with long, snowy winters, with temperatures often falling below minus thirty degrees Celsius (twenty-two degrees Fahrenheit) when the winds and snowstorms blow in from the Baltic Sea, meaning from the north. During this relentless winter, roads became impassable for horse-drawn carriages, and a sled would have to be used instead. Summer was deliciously sunny but never stifling; at long last, life and activity resumed when roads between towns gradually thawed, allowing wagons to once again crisscross the rural thoroughfares. Later, trains began to circulate, but they didn't connect all the cities, and the towns even less so, so roads going to the smallest villages remained the most common transportation routes. Winter typically arrives very early in Lithuania, usually by the latter half of October, and doesn't come to an end before March. It's why we waited impatiently for summer to provide us with sunny days and warmth.

4. The Molotov-Ribbentrop Pact (officially the Treaty of Non-aggression between Germany and the Union of Soviet Socialist Republics) was a neutrality pact between Nazi Germany and the Soviet Union signed in Moscow on August 23, 1939, by Foreign Ministers Vyacheslav Molotov for the Soviet Union and Joachim von Ribbentrop for Nazi Germany. The pact included secret clauses delineating the spheres of interest of the two powers, amended after the invasion of Poland by Germany (in the German-Soviet Frontier Treaty), and remained in force until Adolf Hitler launched the attack on the Soviet Union during Operation Barbarossa on June 22, 1941. This attack marked the beginning of the extermination of the Jews by the Nazi perpetrators, German as well as locals, in Lithuania, as in the Eastern countries.

Born under the Star of May Day

Let's return to my family. In Gorzd (Gargždai), my father, who did not yet speak Lithuanian, went to work with my maternal grandfather, Aaron Meyerowitz. Presumably, Jewish war prisoners of World War I found some relief among the handful of Jewish families living in *shtetlekh*.[1] He later married my mother. My father's second language was Polish, but, like the majority of the Jews of Eastern Europe, his mother tongue, his *mame-loshn*, was Yiddish. Among themselves, Jews reverted naturally and almost exclusively to Yiddish. Most Jews were bilingual, and a lot of Lithuanians who worked with Jews were able to express themselves in Yiddish. Lithuanian is a Baltic, not a Slavic, language and is written in the Roman alphabet. The family remained in Gorzd until I was five, when we moved about fifteen kilometers to Endrejave (Endriejavas, Klaipeda District), a peaceful village of twenty or so wood cabins nestled up against a church, also made of wood.

Endrejave amounted to little more than a lane meandering between flowers and trees. Hidden behind the houses was a small lake where we went swimming. Of the six other Jewish households, two were very close to ours. One of these families had a house that was large enough for everyone, so they gave us two of their rooms.

1. Germany occupied Lithuania and Courland in 1915. Vilnius fell to the Germans on September 19, 1915. Lithuania was incorporated into Ober Ost under a German government of occupation. After the Russian Revolution, the military situation was very complex, and parts of Lithuanian territories changed hands several times until Lithuanian independence.

5

My second brother, Leybe, was born there. Because there was no Jewish school in the village, my older brother stayed in Gorzd to study. Some of the other children attended school in Telz or even went as far away as Memel, which became Klaipeda in 1923. My father, who at first found employment with my grandfather Aaron, was now a foreman with a logging company. In the eyes of the Lithuanian workers, he was a foreigner. Peasants the rest of the year, they found work as seasonal hires in order to make ends meet during the winter months. They brought their own means of haulage and tools to the logging company that employed them. The work consisted first in cutting down the trees and, once the trunks were cleared of branches, sawing them into logs that were then stacked for drying. Indeed, they could not be transported in autumn because the massive wagon wheels would have sunk into the soggy ground. So, paradoxically, it was when the ground had frozen in winter that the logs were loaded onto wagons and were hauled more than twenty kilometers to Klaipeda on the Baltic.

There was an oratory in Endrejave where Jews met at the service times. There were hardly enough attending for a minyan, the minimum number of ten men required to conduct the service. A rebbe[2] taught us the aleph-bet and the rudiments of reading Hebrew in the afternoons. There were barely ten of us in the class, boys and girls together, and I liked one little redheaded girl a lot for her face, which, like mine, was covered in freckles. One day of particular inspiration, with my little classmate, we figured out that we could play doctor. To put our plan into effect, we locked ourselves in the bathroom. But the rebbe quite promptly saw what was amiss. His way of seeing didn't mesh with ours. With due haste, he forced us out of our premises, promptly spelling the end of my first idyll.

We had been living in Endrejave for some time when, one freezing night in the middle of winter, the cowshed caught fire. The

---

2. *Rebbe* and *rov* are used to designate a rabbi, but also in the small communities the teacher, also called the *melamed*.

friends who had sheltered us had a store of food products but also raised livestock and grew some vegetables for market. Half-naked and wrapped in our blankets, we were standing outside while in the cloudless night the sky blazed red. We were lucky the house was spared. But the recollection of the fire that night is engraved in my memory, and I can still see those flames today, as if they are burning before my eyes.

There was no other choice for us but to move to Telz (Telšiai), which we thought of as a major city. Coming from a tiny village, almost a hamlet, and an isolated one at that, everything loomed larger. Relativity affects everything we see. Telz wasn't that large, but it contained an object of pride, a world-renowned yeshiva where students came to study the Talmud from as far away as the United States. Rounding out the list of more modest educational institutions, which contributed toward making Telz a regional center for Jewish learning, was a rabbinic collective, the *kollel*,[3] the Yavne secondary school for girls, and a teachers college for boys, as well as separate boys and girls elementary Jewish schools. In addition to the three main synagogues, there were different prayer rooms, including the one of the tailors and the one called "of the soldiers." The Lithuanians also had their religious institutions. There were two Christian shrines. The Roman Catholic church, an impressive cathedral, overlooked the town from a hill. The other was the beautiful Russian Orthodox church that rose up in the middle of a park and from which you could admire the entire city below, hugging the length of the lake. There were places to rent rowboats along the lake's perimeter for a day's outing on the water. The Lithuanians who lived by the shore engaged in fishing, sometimes relying on their catch for their revenue. They were the ones who sold the fish that the Jews used to buy for *shabbes*, the Sabbath rest, and the holidays. On the outskirts of the city lived more Lithuanians who cultivated large vegetable gardens, while Jews

3. *Kollel*: an institute for full-time, advanced study of talmudic and rabbinic literature. The first *kollel* was founded in Kovno in 1877 by Rabbi Israel Salanter.

tend to inhabit the city center, close to the synagogues and schools, in the maze of streets and alleys that intersected the nearly three-kilometer main street, where the principal businesses could be found.

If not terribly large, Telz was still a very pleasant place to live. In summer we went swimming in the lake, with the men on one side of the lake, of course, and the women having their bathing beach on the other. Bathing suits were not a "required" item, for the simple reason that they were hard to come by in Telz. The two beaches were about a kilometer apart. We boys were all very good swimmers, and none of us hesitated to cross this "no-man's-land" to sneak a peek at the women and girls . . . just to make sure they were observing full decorum. Even as young children we were able to swim the length of the lake and back again. There was a small island right in the middle where we could take a break and catch our breath. To reach this resting place, we would guide ourselves while swimming by following the axis of the church steeple.

In winter the lake was covered with a thick layer of ice. As soon as the snow fell, the wind would sweep it across the flatness, forming drifts here and there. It was inviting to skate on this frozen mirror, as much as we wanted, each of us on one skate—anyone who could afford two was one of the privileged few. When the wind blew, we would open our coats and let it sweep us along and carry us along like giant birds. Pushed by the headier gusts, it took just a few moments to find ourselves three kilometers away, at the other end of the lake. We had to be very careful, however, because the fishermen had the regrettable habit of cutting holes through the ice. Which is how, on a gorgeous day, I plunged into such a dark and frozen abyss from which I was pulled stiff as a board, literally frozen.

The market square offered up a very picturesque and colorful panorama. Its monumental proportions, the architecture and arrangement of the houses, the colors and the generous layout—all combined to produce an artist's tableau. From the Russian Orthodox church standing proudly in the middle of the park, where it stretched along a width of a hundred meters, the square descended and tapered down more than three hundred meters, narrowing to thirty at its lower end. It was a space of imposing dimension. On both sides, the market was lined by Jewish shops, and in the middle, holding court, was an ancient brick building of great distinction that was topped by a gabled roof of red tiles under which were fancy dormer windows. Each window overhung the door of a butcher shop. Whichever side you chose, only kosher butcher shops could be found, each fronted by a long-bearded butcher. A little farther down, a deep well with a heavy crank supplied part of the city's water. The crank had to be turned a long time to raise the bucket. Most people had homes without running water. In the winter the water from the bucket would overflow and create a veritable skating rink; to prevent accidents, sand or cinders had to be spread on the ground. There was a Jewish slaughterhouse on the edge of the city. I never heard of a *Beth-din*, a rabbinical court, in Telz, nor did I ever notice a kosher certificate stamped on any of the items, particularly the meat, unlike what one would see in Paris. In Telz all the butchers were pious Jews, and there was no such thing as a nonkosher butcher.[4]

The streets weren't paved but cobbled with round stones of all different shapes and sizes. Most peasants owned a single horse, and twice a week they drove their horse-drawn wagons to the market. In the winter they supplied the town by sled. For the alleys to remain passable, someone had to be posted in the market square to direct them to a free space, where the horses could be unharnessed and placed quietly behind the wagon. The stalls were packed with every imaginable fruit and vegetable. Chemicals were not used to preserve food. Today's blandness and sterility were instead a perfusion of pleasant and well-differentiated aromas. Live hens and other poultry were to be found as well as the fish needed for *shabbes* and holidays; they were bought, naturally, still alive.

4. *Beth-din*: rabbinical court. Among other functions, it is in charge of ensuring compliance of the food with the Jewish alimentary laws. Probably the rabbis of Telz had a way to certify the kashrut of the meat. There were seventeen butcher shops and cattle traders in the town, twelve (most probably the butchers) held by Jews. See https://kehilalinks.jewishgen.org/telz/telz2.html.

The mistress of every house would bring her poultry to the *shoykhet*, the designated kosher slaughterer prescribed by Jewish law.[5] He used a corner of his own home dedicated to this purpose. The women would then return to their kitchens and pluck the birds, putting the feathers and down aside to make pillows and comforters for winter. They then opened the bird and, if they happened to notice some flaw that might render the bird unfit for consumption, quickly ran to one of the Telzer rabbis to confirm simply that the creature was really kosher.[6]

The majority of Jews lived hand-to-mouth, in poverty. Some could hardly make ends meet, surviving only through constant effort, by undertaking odd jobs to earn their daily bread. Many small craftsmen used a barter system when they were unable to sell their goods. Aside from the occasional wealthy family, there was a very small middle class. But when *shabbes* approached, the entire town began to effervesce, and, no matter if rich or poor, everyone threw themselves into the preparations. Those without means paid on credit, a practice deeply rooted in the local subsistence economy. No contract was signed and no interest charged. One's word was one's bond. The balance that was owed remained open-ended, the merchant recording the article and price only in a notebook or on a piece of paper. The merchant simply deleted his records once he was paid in full. This system had endured a long time and would remain in effect until the war. It goes without saying that *shabbes* for the rich did not resemble *shabbes* for the poor, but as we used to say at home, "a stomach has no windows." No one was supposed to make it his business what others had ingested.

It is relevant at this point of my narrative of the social conditions to mention the proliferation of political parties in Telz, like elsewhere

5. *Shoykhet*: ritual slaughterer. This function was often held by the butcher in the small towns.

6. Rabbis must have served as *mashgiakh*, who was ensuring compliance of the butchers, bakers, and other food businesses with Jewish law.

throughout the Ashkenazic Jewish world. They ran the gamut from organized entities to clubs with three members.[7] It's futile to draw up the whole list, but they fanned out across all platforms and claims on justice, from extreme left to right.

Like every town and village in the world, Telz had its share of the insane and mentally ill people who were simply a little disturbed and never found their place in society. Every single one of them was saddled with a nickname, a label that cast their quirks. Those whose life had bequeathed them some slight flaw or defect were likewise given a nickname and not always a very charitable one. The majority of these individuals surely perished at the hands of the Germans or their Lithuanian collaborators. If, by the greatest of odds, they survived or if their family had only one survivor, I will not here take the chance of offending anyone by naming who was called what.

As I previously mentioned, the Jews lived in the center of the town. When Friday afternoon arrived, a few hours before *shabbes* and the lighting of the candles, each store started to close, one after another, until not a single one remained open and the shtetl was completely emptied. An hour later everyone went to synagogue and, once prayers were over, returned to their homes for the Friday-evening meal. In the city, in spite of the rules imposed by the *shabbes*, it was permitted to carry objects outdoors because the area was inside the perimeter of an *eruv*, to avoid the transgression against carrying, a public practice that still exists in Israel and in places where strong Jewish communities thrive.

Here is how we celebrated the entering of the weekly festival at our typical Lithuanian Ashkenazic house, in a traditional family. Beginning Friday morning, bread for the rest of the week and challah, the sweet plaited buns reserved for *shabbes*, were baked in the house oven, exhaling their aromas. For that matter, everything was

7. At the time of Moishe's life in Gorzd as a child, there was even in this minuscule town an Esperanto club. This universal language was created by Zamenhof at the turn of the century.

homemade, prepared with care, and had the flavor of foods that had simmered a long time. The meal was preceded by the kiddush, the blessing over the wine that was recited on the eve of Sabbath and on the eve of major holidays as well as on the actual days of the holidays. We had a tradition of starting off with herring, either whole or chopped, to whet our appetites. Don't forget that we were less than sixty kilometers from the Baltic Sea, where herring is king. So it was not a luxury item in Lithuania because we could get it thirteen to the dozen at the marketplace. The poor, not being able to provide for themselves with more sophisticated food, depended on the modest price to fill their stomachs with herring and black bread.

But let's get back to the family table on a typical *shabbes* night in a prosperous period. The modest herring appetizer preceded a portion of gefilte fish. The renown of this dish should, in principle, spare me from stating that the fish in question was a carp, although who knows what the stuffed fish will be made from in the future? Today, it is virtually impossible to know what you are being served in the guise of gefilte fish. In those days, the stuffing was most often mixed with the flesh of a pike. As with herring, pike was a common commodity from the lake nearly surrounding the town, whose waters were alive with carp and pike. When the respective fate of the herring and carp had been settled, the *gehakte leber* (chopped liver) made its appearance on the table, and to top off this part of the meal, we still allowed for a fortifying plate of golden broth with homemade noodles (*a teler zup mit lokshn*). And only on Saturday did we attack the main meal, the *tsholnt*, a festive specific dish that was prepared the evening before by a very particular method because of the prohibition against lighting a fire. From Friday evening just before *shabbes* a large stew pot sat in the unkindled yet still hot baker's oven until after Saturday-morning prayers, when each would come to get their dish and bring it home.

The baker was more zealous in studying the Torah than in working at his trade, so we mainly dealt with his wife. Each family would go to pluck their precious creation from the oven, or she brought it to our house at noon on Saturday. All these dishes had a taste . . . I cannot describe—the kishke, made from stuffed goose neck, and the *kneydlekh*, the matzo balls—because the mixture had simmered on a low fire in the wood warm oven for twelve hours or more, and, I hardly dare write it today, the mixture was delectably swimming in fat. Not to mention the *kreplekh*, the chopped meat dumplings that are a miracle of delicacy in the golden broth. In the severe wintry climate, fatty food ensured an efficient protection against the cold and, consequently, held a place of honor at our table. For families that could afford a substantial *shabbes tish*, the Friday-night meal was plentiful but not as heavy as the one we enjoyed at noon on Saturday after services. Who would think about his waistline in such cold? After the *tsholnt*, the traditional dessert was a compote of dried fruits[8] washed down with a glass of cold well water or warm tea. The meal would not be complete without saying the blessing, the Birkat Hamazon, and singing traditional *shabbes* songs.

The old people would then lie down for a little nap, while those who were younger would go out for a walk to help them digest. A few hours before *minha*, the afternoon prayer, the main street became thick with people, even in winter, with icy temperatures. People were just used to the cold, and children went to school in even the coldest weather, which was not considered dangerous. All Jewish stores remained closed, not only on *shabbes* but also the following day, Sunday, which was closing day for Lithuanians.

From the moment of our arrival in Telz, we had lived in a modest-size apartment, set back from the main street near the center of town. Nothing was very far away, and a few minutes were all that was needed to cover the distance that separated downtown from the countryside. The apartment was simple but entirely satisfactory. There was worse, far worse, in our town.

8. Each reader of this text would like to add something here . . . like on good days the traditional *leykekh*, a savory sponge cake.

My father opened a retail fabric shop. It was pretty large and had a very high ceiling so that you had to use a ladder to reach the topmost shelves. My father and mother, and two salespeople, took care of customers. The store was well located, near the spot where the marketplace narrowed. On market days, the peasants and their families flocked to make their purchases, looking for cloth to make curtains and bedcovers, suits and overcoats, or lighter materials to make dresses or aprons. Numerous were those who got their supplies at our store. One must remember that in this period you did not find factory-made clothing. The well-off might occasionally indulge in a bespoke suit made by a tailor or a dress from the dressmaker. Most often, the women were able to sew their own wardrobes. The store also supplied whatever was needed for future young brides and their families to make their trousseaux.

The store did so well that my father opened another one at Naveran, a village about fifteen kilometers from Telz. If the distance was not very great, the road was bad, especially in the spring and fall, when a wagon could barely make the trip. Indeed, it took about three hours to go from Telz to Naveran in the wet season, when boots and wheels sank into the mud. In summer and winter, the trip posed no problem. Worried about how much time was being lost on the way, my father bought a horse, a means of rapid traveling in all seasons that allowed him to keep an eye on the stores. Both stores did well, and, little by little, our lifestyle improved. We rented a spacious house that was equipped with the era's most modern conveniences. It had a courtyard as ample as a football field and a cowshed large enough to accommodate a horse and a cow. It was here, in this courtyard, that I first climbed on a horse at the age of seven. On the Telz scale of things, it was a home that could be taken for a bourgeois residence. Our apartment had five rooms: four bedrooms and a kitchen, which also served as a dining room. There was a small house in the courtyard where a Lithuanian family lived. The husband and wife worked for our landlord, who occupied the other part of the house. The cowshed that housed our horse would soon get another occupant, as my mother decided to buy a cow. From then on we would have fresh milk for the asking, warm and frothy, which I sometimes still dream about.

There was about the same percentage of Russians as Jews in Lithuania. My mother hired a servant, Anna, a prim Russian of about fifty from Lithuania, who took her room and board with us. My mother then "rented" out one bedroom to four *yeshive bokherim*, students at the Talmudic college. The Telz Yeshiva had about four hundred students, and its renown extended far beyond the Lithuanian border. To pay their rent, they taught my older brother and me a page of Gemarah.[9] My mother provided them their *shabbes* meal and, from time to time, one during the week, which was a matter of custom and a mitzvah.[10] In addition to being calm and always soft-spoken, my mother was very pious and strictly observant of Jewish law. My father, on the other hand, was not at all observant, even though I remember him chanting from memory the kiddush, the blessing over the wine, on *shabbes* eves without needing the prayer book. He had a beautiful voice. But like most of his friends, he identified himself more with Zionism. They were nonreligious Zionists who came from the middle and sometimes wealthy classes. Among them was the writer Yankel Rabinovitch,[11] who later emigrated to Canada. From a political point of view, he was the spearhead of this small group. After the war he remained a friend of my father and visited him several times in Paris. When I was once again reunited with him, my father owned an important library of around five hundred Yiddish books. My father read mostly in Yiddish, and, besides, in

9. Gemarah: page of the Talmud comprising rabbinical analysis and commentaries.

10. Mitzvah: good deed, generally one prescribed by the law.

11. I recently had the unexpected and good fortune to meet with Gila Fortinsky, the granddaughter of Yankel (Ya'akov) Rabinovitch, thus confirming many details from my father's account. His book, *Bleter fun Yidish Lite* (Tel Aviv: Hamenora Publishing House, 1974), has now been digitized in the NYPL-Yiddish Book Center Yizkor Book Collection. https://www.yiddishbookcenter.org/collections /yizkor-books/yzk-nybc314148.

Lithuania the Zionists carried their propaganda in Yiddish. When Jabotinsky[12] came to Telz to hold a conference, it was the language in which he expressed himself, just as he always did when he proselytized in Lithuania.

Once a week, this group would get together at one of the households to play cards until the wee hours of the morning. Their two favorite games were poker and seventy, a popular game back then. Money was not really the main motivation to play but provided the required excitement. With the exception of the mistress of the house in charge of hosting, who took care of the preparations and serving food and drink all night, women were not present at these parties. Need I add that the other wives did not always appreciate their husbands' recreations? It fell to one or another to dramatically demonstrate their annoyance, here breaking a window and there provoking an outburst in order to express her bitter feelings. Without doubt, they sometimes had good reason to revolt. Among the men there were those who did not content themselves with cards. Where they would go, I was never able to say for certain, but rumors did circulate. So it wasn't rare for one of the wives to come looking for her husband and force the unlucky one out of the party under a constant stream of invectives from his better half. These scandals didn't really change anything, and, in the end, life went on more or less the same way . . .

I want to pause here and slip in an episode that I did not mention in the Yiddish version of this text, out of modesty toward my children and grandchildren, but even more so because I was afraid to cause pain to my younger sister. That being said, it is important to talk about it, no matter how painful it may be, because it is true to the reality and accounts for our situation as a family. When his businesses were both thriving, my father found a girlfriend, a cousin of my mother and a beautiful girl. At first, they went out on the sly, but gradually people began noticing and talking, and the talk about the

---

12. Vladimir Ze'ev Jabotinsky (1880–1940), a prolific writer, was a controversial figure in the history of Zionism, and theoretician of nationalism.

affair got around. I was little more than seven years old, and my first instinct was to try to safeguard my father's reputation and honor. But everyone eventually found out. Secrets did not remain secrets for long, and tongues began to wag. At that point the story took a different turn. One evening, when I knew they would be outside the movie house, I lay in wait for them on the street. I wasn't about to receive them with honors or flowers. What I flung right at their faces was horse dung, freshly picked. The incident went no further. If I had been older, I might have pursued a plan of action, a strategy or a tactic, in terms both military and political. But I was only a kid, and nothing I did was ever premeditated. Waiting out their appearance from the theater took all my attention. The rest just came to me with the instinct of a seven-year-old child, without any thought. Of course, my father never made any mention of this unfortunate episode, neither then nor later. To my mother I said nothing, and if she ever did find out, it hadn't come from my own mouth. She was probably aware, however, for everything was known, as I've said before. Nobody ever broached the subject at home. What other means had I, a child, to protest or to express my feelings? Of course, today I see things differently, but when we're children, our actions just come to us, and I was going to revolt.

In those days television didn't exist, but we already had two movie houses in Telz. For some, this was the chosen way to kill time, while others played dominoes. The faith and dedication it took to squint through a page of sacred text were not for everyone. This was even true for well-read people, such as my father, who was not unfamiliar with the small-font commentaries in the Talmud, as was his own father, Mozes Rozenbaum, who was a rabbi in Warsaw. But in Telz, with God as my witness, not everyone followed the new trends. The town was full of men carrying beards and many others who stuck to simple observance (*stam frum*), though they showed no outward signs of faith. No less than other towns and villages of Lithuania, Telz had nothing to feel ashamed about.

I began my schooling at a *kheyder*, a Jewish primary school. If I certainly cannot boast of having been a good student, the reason is not that I was empty-headed. My abilities were entirely normal. But I loved horsing around and making jokes. I had a lot of energy, so I was often punished by being sent to the corner, face turned to the wall, or, worse yet, sent outside the door. How could I be expected to spend most of my time outside the classroom and learn anything properly? But in spite of everything, during these years I did manage to learn to read and to count.

Of all my teachers, only one really left his mark on me: he happened to be the religious instructor. May he forgive me, and may he rest in peace in the other world. Even though there was nothing extraordinary about his physical appearance, this melamed frightened me. He seemed to come right out of one of those long-ago fables. He was probably not more than forty-five or fifty years old, but a child could easily think he was much older. His beard was as black as coal, and his very dark eyes had the same glare as those cherries found only in the Baltic countries. Decked out in a shiny suit whose four buttons were always closed, and wearing a perpetual tie, he nevertheless had a neglected appearance. His bowler hat was too tall, made from an unusual and stiff material. And he never took it off. What's more, he never let go of the ruler that he held in his hand. When a pupil began to read, he would follow line after line with the point of the fearsome ruler. If, God forbid, the poor child made a mistake, the ruler left the page and fell down on the errant finger. This was one of his teaching methods, but there was more to his pedagogy. If a more serious error was made, he ordered the unfortunate student to lower his pants down to his underwear, and he would take off his belt and start spanking. When he thought the guilty party's behind was sufficiently red, he stopped. Several days were needed before the poor kid was able to sit down again without pain. What could a child do, faced with this man straight out of mythology? The children would try any means to avenge themselves. Everyone had his own way of reacting. My particular stock in trade was to put a candle in the stove in the middle of winter. This calls for a little explaining. In Lithuania we warmed ourselves with firewood. One of these stoves had the capacity to heat two or three rooms, sometimes more. Made of brick, they were covered with earthenware tiles, which, once the wood had burned off, would slowly release the heat from the coals. All you had to do was throw a candle into the stove to produce a cloud that was so choking that everyone had to leave the classroom, promoting a general evacuation. We could then play and let off steam in the big enclosed courtyard, where I felt like a fish in water.

I had one other specialty. While still very young, I understood the principles of electricity and had a real interest in it. Even today, I find electrical work alluring. I will gladly perch myself atop a stepladder and won't balk at getting flat on my stomach for some delicate repair in my own or my children's houses. It seems like I did my apprenticeship in my mother's belly. So I exercised my talents by causing short circuits, and in a country where nightfall in winter begins at three in the afternoon, it was difficult for classes to continue without electricity. We were always up to these kinds of pranks and practical jokes. For as long as childhood lasts, this headstrong attitude flatters one's vainglory, but looking back on it now, these incidents make me cringe a little.

I got on well with my other teachers, but I had a special respect for our gym instructor. We played football and other sports, but more than anything else, our favorite thing was fighting. Boys love to test their strength, and in our school, where we were only boys, at the drop of a hat we would go at each other to be top dog. Here's what our drill was: We teamed up with a few friends so that we could assault another team of friends. Once the brawling started, no quarter would be given. I must admit to not having disliked this and, frankly, to have gone for it. Many of the mothers came to denounce me and complain to my mother about my conduct, and, being very just, she would reply in her calm voice that she would take the necessary measures and see to my punishment. I certainly deserved to be given a lesson, but I was only a child, and my mother treated me as such. She knew perfectly well how to distinguish good from evil. "Meyshele," she would say, "all this fighting makes no sense. You have to live in peace with your fellows. It isn't good. You have to stop all this foolishness." And I promised her it would never happen again, saying, "I swear to you." Unfortunately, our conversation was quickly forgotten. My older brother, Yosef, took after our mother and was a very composed young man. He worked hard at school, conducted himself as an exemplary student, and associated with decent people. With him my mother didn't have many reasons to worry.

Winters were very cold, and I remember getting very sick with the flu or a sore throat, I can't remember which, after we had moved into our new apartment. I had a high temperature and very little appetite, so my mother gave me some money, but on one condition: I had to promise to eat better. On a day when she had gone out, I started to count up my small fortune, and it turned out that I was rich enough to buy myself some real ice skates. Like most other kids, I used to make my own skates from wood. My dream was to own real ones, but I never had enough money, and here it was: it seemed like I was there; the chance to skate on two metal blades was finally at hand. I got dressed in a hurry and ran to the hardware store, two hundred meters from our house. I asked for the best pair, the shiniest ones. They shone like a mirror before my eyes. I was already picturing myself on the ice. The owner of the store looked at me carefully over his glasses and asked me if I had money. My head barely reached the counter. I had my little nest egg with me and gleefully emptied it before his eyes. Without any further ado, he took a pair of brand-new, shimmering skates off the shelf. He was about to wrap them up, but I immediately stopped him. I had to put them on right away. Understand that in those days, skates were sold without boots and were screwed on with a key. I left the store and, in the blink of an eye, covered the distance between the store and our house. The road was quite suitable for sliding, recently covered with snow that had been made very hard by sleds passing over it. With hardly any time to get out of my clothes, I had to rush, throwing myself all dressed under the covers with the two skates still screwed onto my shoes before my mother opened the door to the house. The first thing my mother did, naturally, was to look in on her patient. When she saw my face, all flushed, it was a catastrophe. She put her hand on my forehead and let out an "*A brokh iz mir*!" (Woe is me!). My head was burning like bread straight from the oven, and I was bathed in sweat under the covers. She was already talking about calling the doctor. I tried to calm her down, but I could see that she was still alarmed. The idea came to her to touch my feet, inaccessible and covered with their armor. When she understood that I was all dressed and wearing my skates, she calmly but firmly commenced her inquiry. I had no choice but to admit everything. She took off my shoes and, taking the offending objects with her, went to the store owner and manifested her unhappiness. She absolutely could not understand how someone could have sold skates to a child less than seven years old who more-over had even come in all alone! She was quietly refunded and came back home. Throughout the episode, my mother never betrayed any trace of unkindness, but she promised to take measures after my recovery. In the meantime, she had forgiven me, and after I got better she actually took me to buy the pair of skates I had coveted so much.

In the free time of my childhood I really loved playing football. The kids would meet on a sort of vacant lot where the grass had actually just been cut, close to downtown. All around the lot amid the high grass cattle were grazing. Netless goals were distinguished by two posts and marked the field's boundaries. We formed two teams . . . knowing that we didn't always have the right number of players, but we at least tried to equalize the teams facing each other and in this way had a good time. From this child's game came some dedicated players who would later join the adult teams, which would be my case. I loved sports! I had learned to swim by the age of four in a country with so many lakes and rivers that the boys went swim-ming without adults and learned to swim like fish without ever hav-ing a single lesson. Water was a kind of natural milieu, and I did not often hear talk of drowning.

There was one other activity that was particularly dear to me, although I don't know that it can be classified as a sport. I got into the habit of visiting the orchards where all kinds of fruits were to be found. My family didn't own one, but there were orchards in abundance all around, everywhere in and around Telz. Fruit was sold cheaply. The peasants drove the wagons into town, buckling under the weight of fruits and vegetables. The produce was sold not by the kilo but by liters, one or two or five. The peasants made use of another unit of measure, the *dvolika*, corresponding to a sixteen-liter (four-gallon) bucket. Of all the fruits, my favorite by far, which has never changed, was the apple, the way they were when picked from the tree, so tasty and crunchy, from their skin to their core, until nothing was left but the wooden stem. I've continued to eat them like this all my life and have always, thank God, been able to perfectly digest them. But I have never again found that same feeling of delight that I experienced when I pulled the fruit from its branch and, right there, took that first crunchy bite. Its taste was incomparable. I realized only later that it wasn't only the flavor of the fruit that I was savoring but the taste of childhood itself. The feeling of delight was inseparable from the risk. We always took a risk in the orchard, but there was less of a risk if we went over the wall (well, not really a wall, but a small fence of wood planks). We would push one aside to make our discreet opening at the bottom and close it up again as though nothing had occurred after we had ingested our booty. But all orchards did not find favor in my eyes. To tell the truth, I preferred going solo, even if I occasionally pulled a "job" with friends. In that case, I was in charge. We liked raiding the best orchards, which happened to be the most guarded ones, an experience that I relied on greatly later on in the army. Our choice of an orchard would be contingent on the risks. The more there were, the more we liked it. The big orchard of the Catholic seminary or the Orthodox priest's remained our favorites. When my family moved for a third time, the priest became our neighbor, but I will discuss this later.

Our expeditions did not always end with success. Sometimes the seminarians ran after us, but because they were encumbered by their long robes, we usually ran faster than they did. One day, operating solo, I was caught by the owner, who took my cap as hostage. Unfortunately, it was the one my mother had given me as a present for Shavuot.[13] If I had wanted to offend God, I wouldn't have known how to find a better way to do it. I was ashamed—what a great sin I had committed! Finally, my mother negotiated and successfully recovered my new cap. My remorse probably indicated that I had a penchant for religion, but for me to understand that and to fulfill the yearning took me another fifty years under incentives that were entirely different. By then, I had done a lot of thinking and had made a long journey. It wasn't that I was an atheist in my childhood, although I did become one later when I began working. I simply tended to follow my own impulses. I would act without thinking. If we return to the story of the stolen apples, in this context religion was colored by a rather pejorative feeling, given that its materialization was a Catholic seminary and a Russian Orthodox priest.

These little thefts were more or less commonplace among the youth of Telz. But thinking more carefully about it, although we were stealing fruit, we were not making a profit, but simply eating it on the spot. It is written in the Torah: "You will hand over a portion of your field or your orchard to the poor, the orphaned, and the widowed." None of us was rich, and I was, in a certain sense, from the age of eight, orphaned from my father. And if there were no widows among us, well, it seemed we had no confidence in the owners, and still less the clergy, to hand over the least part of their orchards to us.

Most of the Jews from Lithuania were exterminated. According to historians, 95 percent of this population was annihilated. After the war, survivors organized into associations (*landsmanshaftn*) named after their hometowns to pay tribute to the Jewish population of the city or the town in which they lived before the war. They often contributed to commemorative works (*yizker bikher*) about their city or region. All these books were written after the Holocaust in

13. Shavuot: Jewish festival held on the sixth and seventh of the month of Sivan, fifty days after the second day of Passover. Originally a harvest festival, it commemorates the giving of the law (the Torah).

memory of the lost communities. The authors describe their past, tell the history of their lost families, and publish old photographs. They glorify the purity, the morality, and especially the piety of the men and women who lived there. Most of such works were published in either Israel or the United States. The authors, survivors, or family often speak to former dwellers of such towns or their descendants who might want to purchase a copy. That's how I bought a copy of the *yizker bukh* for the town of Telz, *Sefer Telz*. The authors did their best to emphasize the most praiseworthy aspects of life there. The piety of most Jewish inhabitants was remarkable and measured up to other Lithuanian cities, as I've already discussed. Like any number of other towns in Lithuania, such as Ponevezh, Slobodke, or others, Telz had its share of holiness. Although to be accurate, if we really want to be objective and honest, we have to acknowledge that among the Jewish population of the town, there were very pious families, moderately religious ones, and some complete atheists. In Telz they were careful to not offend the religious and would refrain from working, smoking, or riding a bicycle on *shabbes*. Cars were not a factor. This aspect of Jewish life was not accounted for in the Telz *yizker bukh*, nor did it evoke the poverty and misery that were so prevalent.

A portion of the population lived in conditions that were tragic. Many lived in cellars or in basement lodgings. At the mercy of the cold that gripped the winter and the suffocating heat of summer, without electricity, their only daylight was accessible from whatever broke through a small window atop a street-level wall. To see the sun or sky, they had to somehow manage to peek up through that window. The floors were of beaten earth. Their only nourishment was one piece of black bread and a bit of powdered sugar to dig their teeth into. Most of these shelters had a single room lit with a tiny kerosene lamp. A stove that did a very bad job of heating was also used to cook soup. Miserably clothed, sometimes even in rags, this impoverished segment of society contained the pious, the atheists, and Gentiles mixed in among them. This category of the population constituted the *lumpenproletariat* surviving on low-paying day jobs, who were far from being caught up in the revolutionary consciousness that had won over the workers in the big cities and towns. I think every family in Telz was more or less closely connected to these residents living under such horrible conditions. We must know the truth of all sides of our story, both the saddest and the best parts. It is the other side of the coin. I myself have been to some of these cellars and tasted their black bread dipped in sugar. There must still be some survivors from this period who now live in an entirely different country and in another world, who enjoy the consumer society but remember the Old World sufferings. We have not spoken enough of the common folk, the artisans and *balagoles* (cart drivers, coachmen), who broke their backs to earn their daily bread, not getting enough to eat, struggling to survive from one day to the next and still not satisfying their hunger. This Telz existed also. We mustn't delude ourselves thinking that the inhabitants of the city all belonged to the upper crust. Not everyone was descended from aristocracy or the religious or intellectual elite. And that does not mean there is any reason to be ashamed of the city or an incentive to examine only a portion of the population. On the contrary, our history is not aggrandized by an idealized representation. The fact is that everyone knew each other because all in all we lived in a pretty small town. What fate had for each one, good or bad, was not in our hands. To my eyes, tribute is paid to the city and its inhabitants when seen through its true features, by remembering who we really were without leaving anything in the shadows, even if today it all seems a very long way from who we are now. The lives of the poor are no less worthy of remembering and memory than the "highborn." It is a part of our families' story, and it must not disappear.

Both of my father's stores were doing very well, but his time to get rich hadn't come yet. The skies were darkening. A black cloud was coming from the other side of the Atlantic. Like a hurricane sweeping everything in its path, the world economic crisis found its way into our small Lithuanian city. When the abrupt drop in sales began to make itself felt, he was forced to sell his second store and the horse, just to survive. The horse was not needed in Telz since the store was only steps from the house. In spite of these measures, we still had to limit our lifestyle in order to reduce expenses. The sacrifices were still not enough to cope with our expenses or to pay the bills. The bank refused to grant the easy terms they had granted when business was better. In a word, everything was vanishing and being taken away. Caught in this first storm, we had no inkling that what would follow the economic crisis would be even worse.

It was unlike today, when a businessman can file for bankruptcy while beginning to suspend payments without being declared in default and do these things sometimes while creating another company and so go back to his work. At the time, in a small city like Telz, the business was simply declared bankrupt, and the casualty would get the lifelong label of *bankrutshnik*, with which you were stigmatized until the end of your days. What's more, you were deemed responsible and brought to court. My father was seeing everything he had built crumble beneath his feet and his business go over a cliff. He saved everything he possibly could. He hid some fabric in some peasants' homes, packed up his bags, and made quickly for Paris, where he had a sister.

Der broyt geber, the Breadwinner

In the thirties, even before my father left, we had to leave our "bour-geois" apartment that we could no longer afford and find more mod-est accommodations. We were now three boys, and my mother was expecting a fourth child that my father never got to know. She never uttered the slightest criticism of my father in our presence, nor did she complain that he didn't write or send us any money. The dig-nity she demonstrated was unfailing. My youngest brother and the fourth of us was born in Telz in 1931. We named him Elie, not only after Eliyahu Hanavi, Elijah the Prophet, but because it was a Jewish tradition to remember a deceased relative. We all had biblical first names, including for Leybe (the lion), which embodies strength in the Bible and although—or because—our Leybe, the third brother, was pretty scrawny. We were four boys, Yosef (Joseph), Moishe (Moses), Leybe, and Elie, similar to so many other boys in Jewish families, our names taken from the Bible or from close family members who had passed on. But henceforth we would deviate from the typical Jewish family.

The last apartment we occupied before the war had four rooms and a kitchen. It was located in the first house on the main street, on the market square, opposite my father's former store and close to the Orthodox church and its park. Telz was built on small hills—on the scale of such a flat country—no more than fifty or a hundred meters high. All the way down along the three-kilometer banks were the homes of our Lithuanian neighbors who were mainly fishermen. Perched more or less sixty meters above them, on the first cliff road, was the next row of larger houses. They were well-built wooden

houses embellished by windowed sunrooms that offered a great panorama on the lake. Hiking up another forty meters or so, you were
on the main street, which coursed parallel to the lake. Our house was
at the far end and looked out onto the market square and the lake
below. The main thoroughfare continued above and parallel to the
lake into the marketplace extension, changing names a few times,
climbing and descending the city's hills until it headed out of the city
and toward the plains. At one end of the marketplace, the Catholic
church occupied the summit, while opposite and slightly below, sitting enthroned in the park, was the Russian Orthodox church. Our
apartment was one of two on the first floor of our new house. We
were boarders, while the landlord occupied the other apartment. The
attic contained a garret and two other rooms. There was a very large
cellar that filled with enough water in summer to sail a boat, while
in winter the icy spread could be skated on. The house was right
next to the park on the hill dominated by the small Russian Orthodox church, from which the view of the lake and its little island was
unimpeded. In the middle of the park was a pedestal on which stood
an old impressive cannon, although I'm not able to say during which
war it had been used. Like the other buildings on our side of the main
street, the back of our house leaned against a slope. In the front, you
had to climb three steps to reach the entrance, while in the back,
you entered on porch level onto a veranda, where we used to erect
our hut for the eight days of the Sukkoth festival. A hallway opened
there where my mother stored all sorts of things she made, like goose
fat, jam, and several kinds of canned goods for the long winter. Our
poverty was such that she made her own preserves out of red beets
that she found for almost nothing and hardly needed sweetening.
The closet was never locked.

I don't know why I'm relating all this in such detail. Perhaps it
seems like I'm trying to sell that apartment. For sure, my childhood
home fills me with profound nostalgia, the very same home I walked
away from one day and returned to find not a soul alive.

In the courtyard, there was a granary, with a respectably sized
silo where wheat and barley were stored. From the top, a large

conduit emptied the grain directly into bags, ready to be sold. The owners were two Jewish partners. On one side of the granary was a space allotted to us, and we needed it because the cow was among the possessions we had saved from our debacle. The courtyard was enormous. At the far end was a garden of fruits and vegetables that belonged to another Lithuanian who grew them for sale in the market. The vegetable garden was no more than twenty-five meters wide but stretched out along a length of more than three hundred meters. The city and the country were merging everywhere. Our house was right next to the vegetable garden, and the vegetable garden was right next to the orchard of the bishop whom I wrote about earlier. A jump over the garden fence brought me into the orchard, and, you know . . . I wasn't going there to be baptized. Lover of apples and pranks that I was, the orchard had long since become like my second home.

Following the marketplace and walking downhill I was in five minutes at the lake where I loved to swim. From our house, we just had to cross the street, climbing a few steps to be in the park. The view was magnificent there, looking out over the houses and the panorama of the lake and town. If it were only up to appearances, this could all seem charming enough. And when a family is privileged enough to have a cow and a maid to boot, what was there to complain about?

All of this beauty and charm of the nature surrounding us were certainly very real, but it was only the deceptive reflection that sparkled on the surface. We were in fact four orphans. Nobody has the right to say so while one's father is alive, but that's how much I resented him and the way I perceived my existence. What's more, my mother had a heart condition. We also had to find a solution to my grandfather's housing situation. My grandmother Tsivia had had an accident descending the cellar stairs and could no longer get out of bed. Sometime later she died in Gorzd. My mother's hometown was located fifty kilometers from Telz and no more than ten kilometers from the Baltic Sea. The only thing we had to do was to take Grandfather to come live with us.

So here was a household full of eaters. Including the maid, there were now seven mouths to feed, my mother, my grandfather, the maid, and four boys, without starving the cow. The most mundane daily issues became insurmountable problems. It is almost uncanny what a stomach can demand. When you are eating your fill and living normally, even if modestly, there is no way to realize just how succulent the simplest dishes can be. But when you know hunger, you no longer ask what there is to eat, only how you are going to fill your empty belly. It only gets more complicated when the prospect of coming into any money is nil. Grandfather suffered from nose cancer and had stopped working. He needed constant care and had to undergo frequent operations, which added up to a lot of money, especially because he constantly had to travel to Berlin, where there was advanced plastic surgery.

Under these conditions, our situation was worsening by the day. Whatever stockpiles we had were becoming scarce. They were at the point of evaporating and then totally vanishing. Our household was hardly recognizable. From the material my father had hidden away with some peasants, we managed to recover only a part, but their fruits took a very circuitous route to our stomachs. Our only remaining asset was the cow, and though she gave us delicious and precious milk that produced excellent things like fresh cream and butter, there was no more bread to butter. My mother decided to first fix the short-term problems and then tackle the long-term ones. In order to better manage the economic crisis we faced, she decided to sell the cow, but soon this income also dried up. To tighten our belts one more notch, she decided to give notice to Anna, our maid. Anna had been a part of the family, like home furniture. But unlike old furniture, she was outspoken. In Yiddish she pleaded with my mother, reminding her that she had raised us, washed and dressed us, that she knew how to prepare kosher meals and bake bread and the *shabbes* challah. All she asked for was a piece of bread and a place to sleep. My mother finally told herself that confronting famine with six or seven mouths to feed made no big difference: we would starve in either case. She yielded to her pleas, so Anna then remained with us for ten more years, right up until the war. Meanwhile, our situation never stopped deteriorating, to the point of becoming really unbearable.

Very much in spite of ourselves, we now resorted to a strictly vegetarian diet. We were eating what the Russians called *poshlost*, or *poshnou*, a soup made from a stock of the cheapest market vegetables. Our foods had become tasteless and were cooked without any fat. The recipe for *poshnou* was simple enough: take a pot and fill it almost to the top with water, add a few noodles, one or two potatoes, half a glass of barley, and a little salt and pepper. When it starts to boil, sit down at the table and, when you eat, try hard to forget your hunger and focus your attention on images of meat or other delicious dishes. Those were gone now from our house but remained in our dreams. Even the very affordable fish of Telz was too expensive for us. From my father there came nothing to relieve our misfortunes. Zushe, my mother's brother in South Africa, sent a few pounds once in a while, though too rarely to make a difference in everyday life. Her two sisters in America would send packages of used clothes, but these were, unfortunately, inedible. Butchers who had known my mother in better times with her scrupulous honesty and decency suggested that she take their meat on credit, but she most often turned down the offer, well aware that she could not repay the debts. She began to think and put each of us under review: Who among us was able to go out and work and bring a few pennies into the house? Yosef was three years older than I was and proved to be a very good student; he was a candidate for the teachers college. Leybe was only nine, and Elie was still very small. Grandfather was too old, and my mother was sick.

Her survey was quickly concluded: I was the only member of the family who could go out to work. Yes, the only one meant to become a proletarian was me, as destiny made me see the light on May 1, the traditional Labor Day. If that is not a symbol . . . Besides, I was not among the students who wore themselves out studying. My schooling was over with by the age of ten and a half, when my mother placed me as an apprentice to a photographer. Isn't it a beautiful profession? It was for all appearances a good job that would provide a skill, with a promising flavor of art. But it seems not have been in God's plans to make of me an artist. The boss began teaching me the trade. He made me retouch the plates in pencil—well, not completely, as he did most of the finishing off himself. Mainly, we retouched the eyebrows, the eyes, the shape of the lips and the nose, working directly on the plates, since rolls of film didn't exist yet. We could shorten the nose without need of plastic surgery. This was particularly useful for young women whose parents had entrusted a matchmaker with finding a husband. Many families still married their poor but studious boys to girls whose parents could afford the young man's schooling. The groom would meet his fiancée (and vice versa) for the first time at the very moment of the ceremony. Each snapshot was memorialized on a glass plate, changed after every exposure. After retouching what needed retouching, the boss made me work in the darkroom for several hours because he found I was resourceful. My boss taught me to develop the pictures while counting evenly in Yiddish up to *ein-un-tsvantsik* (twenty-one). That was our stopwatch. After that, the pictures had to be placed in a water bath for washing and then hung to dry. Everything transpired in the darkroom. Imagine yourself, a ten-year-old kid, in a room of total blackness! I was not exactly a coward, but the more I stayed in that room, the more afraid I became, which is how I missed my vocation and became neither photographer nor artist. My mother was sorry about the six wasted months. Without delay, we had to figure out a new career.

Since our wardrobe was getting shiny from being overworn and there was no money for a new one, my mother got the idea of talking to a tailor who specialized in salvaging old clothes. The key part of his work was turning the material inside out. His fees were judiciously calculated, to appeal to the poorest of the poor. My mother could not allow herself to dress four boys in new clothes, and this justified her decision to seize the first chance of placing me into an apprenticeship with a tailor and, better yet, one who knew how to restore garments. Perhaps you don't know what is involved. The work consisted of taking a pair of pants or any clothing and disassembling them by completely unpicking all the stitching, cleaning up the seams by removing all the threads with a blade, and finally, after having ironed the clothes on the used side, passing the iron over the side that had been the lining and would, from now on, be on the outside. That the pocket changed sides during the procedure was of little importance. This time, God decided to bestow his grace on me, because in less than the six days that he needed to create the world, I became a tailor, from which there was no going back!

The impoverishment of the tailor was outstanding. His family lived in a lightless dwelling that was located in the basement of a very beautiful, newly built wood house, owned by a dentist. His home consisted of two pathetically small bedrooms that were lit by weak light coming through the cellar windows that looked out on the lake. The view was splendid, but the same could not be said of the accommodations. One of the two rooms served as the workshop, and the other was a bedroom where the entire family, parents and children, crammed together to sleep. To appreciate the situation, you must understand that there were about ten children, from the oldest, who was twenty or so, to the youngest, a girl, not older than four years. Under these conditions, you will understand why it would be unfair to call the head of this family, with his miserable appearance and lifestyle, "the boss." He was a puny man, poorly clothed, with a reddish complexion and a goatee of the same color. His wife was a minuscule figure who wore disheveled clothes as much as her hair was unkempt. She spent her time engaging in recriminations and screaming, demanding money to go on some errands. And this was precisely the rub. Of the money, the tailor didn't often have much to hand over, and when he had any, it was never enough. Instead of handing over the money she demanded, he hurled a volley of invectives at her, but rarely did he have the last word. In the charm department, his wife easily defeated him and proved herself far more refined than he was. She answered cursing with far more vehement substance and insults that were a hundred times worse. It was right out of a Sholem Aleichem story.[1]

When I arrived in the morning, the first "job" I was given was—I apologize for mentioning it—emptying his chamber pot. In those days there were neither toilets nor bathrooms in the homes, and even running water was fairly rare. That first chore completed, I picked up the broom and did my best to get rid of the dust in the two family rooms where the family was crammed together. There were not parquet or even cement floors, but ones made of clay. It is remarkable that one might well be a *shnorer* (a poor man relying on the charity of individuals or the community) and still ape bourgeois manners and exploit a weaker one. So what could a poor eleven-year-old kid do other than to obey? In a small corner of the workshop that was reserved for the kitchen, there was an iron stove where the family cooked their meals and prepared the charcoal meant for the use of the flatiron that, needless to say, was not electric. The fuel needed to be placed in the forge and then blown upon to keep the embers lit and stoked. That was my next job, but at eleven years old my lungs were not yet as developed as those of an adult, and my efforts turned out to be entirely insignificant. Next, I went to the well, fifty meters below the house, for water. The reader has every right to wonder what these jobs had to do with the apprenticeship of a tailor. Well, at the time, things were like that. It was only once these tasks were finished that I had access to a needle, if then. They were more willing to trust me with the knife so that the old clothes could be unstitched (while carefully avoiding slashing them) and then the job of cleaning up the threads or ironing. The needle represented a more advanced stage of the learning process. At first, I had to simulate the movement, stitching a piece of material with an unthreaded needle. It was

1. Sholem Aleichem (Shalom Rabinovitz [1859–1916]), one of the founding fathers of modern Yiddish literature. A master of Jewish humor and of the spoken Yiddish idiom, Sholem Aleichem carved the modern archetypes, myths, and fables of the Eastern European Jewish world. See http://www.yivoencyclopedia .org/article.aspx/Sholem_Aleichem.

called "grasping the needle." I will not further enumerate or describe the entirety of operations that I had to become familiar with to learn the tailor's craft. To become a tailor, I traveled a road as long as the list of my bosses. And maybe even longer to become a fine artisan. I stayed less than a year with this first tailor. Telz had about ten others, among whom were good ones, mediocre ones, and really bad ones. They all had, especially those with the least talent, nicknames.

My second employer was short and especially well developed width-wise. He was among the inexpensive tailors, though he sewed new clothes only. His clients were people of rather modest means or peasants from the surrounding countryside. Customarily, before executing an order, the tailor takes a client's measurements. But this man was satisfied just to size the customer at a glance and memorize the proportions. And it was this memorized image that probably guaranteed the "precision" of his work. Unfortunately, when fabric is cut according to guesswork, the results are occasionally unexpected, and if that turned out to be the case and the swath was too large, the tailor would maintain to the client that the material would shrink, or if it happened to have turned out to be too tight, well, then it would stretch. His work was also coarse, done with wide stitching to save time and with sloppy finishing touches rushed by machine when what was demanded was delicate hand-stitching. The man had three daughters who were several heads taller than he was and as heavy as bears. They had nothing to be ashamed of either in regards to their width, and so they waited quite a while before they married. It was there, with my second boss, that I earned my first *litas* (Lithuanian money). Despite the modest sum, I proudly brought it to my mother because the income was very useful. My first pay was enough to buy bread and sugar for the whole family.

I left this boss for a third, then a fourth, and so kept changing them often. At the age of fourteen, I had become *der broyt geber*, the family support, and was earning almost an adult salary. Despite my young age, I didn't punch a clock or receive a regular schedule and stayed at work late into the night. I finally ended up working for someone who had several workers in his workshop and was up-to-date with the times. Strictly speaking, he was not a very good tailor, but he understood that he could not easily make a living by doing it all by hand. He was no fool, of course, but he didn't care to know whether the work he did was beautiful. The only thing that mattered was knowing how much the task at hand would bring in. He clothed wealthy peasants and people of some means. It still wasn't manufacturing in the sense we understand it today. But he had understood the principle of the assembly line and was the wealthiest tailor in town. He owned the beautiful home that he lived in, surrounded by a large orchard whose plum trees yielded fruit of a size and taste I have never experienced since. When you entered the gate, a long lane lined with rose bushes on both sides led to a magnificent veranda. The house contained a ground floor and one above it with many rooms. The boss had been a friend of my father's, and in better times he had been a regular visitor at our house and my father would also visit him. His house was as busy as a hive. Rare luxury at the time, a radio broadcast music and news all day into the living room where customers waited in armchairs. There was not such a device in our house. It was through this radio that I first heard Hitler's baying against the Jews in 1934 or 1935. We were less than sixty kilometers from Germany and understood the language perfectly.

There was an incessant coming and going in the house that brought it to life, and when night had fallen, you would still find yourself there playing cards, like my father had done when he was a habitué. The regulars would drink and eat roasted duck and a lot of other things. The party went on late into the night, and to me it seemed like that was the good life. Among all my bosses, this was the one with the most cosmopolitan and secular attitudes. I was only an observer, like the others working there, among whom were two Lithuanians, which was pretty rare in the shop of a Jewish tailor.

I had become an adult over the course of time and ended up leaving this well-loved boss. But I continued to pay him visits because he had shown me such exceptional kindness, whether out of sympathy for my family circumstances or simply out of loyalty to my father.

I have to tell you that I was never let go by any of my bosses. I was the one who left of my own free will when I decided to. According to a Yiddish expression that seems custom-made for tailors, I had needles, *shpilkes*, in my behind. I was fidgety. There were a couple of reasons for it. First of all, I always wanted to improve, to become an expert, and also I was looking to earn more money for my family's needs.

I'll skip over several jobs to finish up this period and talk about my last boss with whom I stayed up until the Russian army entered Lithuania in 1940. There I held the job of an adult worker and was paid as such, and it was there that I truly learned my craft. While all my other bosses had been men's tailors, this one made clothes mostly for women. To me he was the best tailor in the city and the region, gifted with real talent and truly proficient at his craft. In addition, he had a very endearing family with several children. The two eldest sons worked with their father. I felt as at home with them as I did in my own family and was completely devoted to them. He was so well known that whoever came in to order an item of clothing had to come armed with patience.

In those days, the customer brought in the fabric himself: the lining, thread, minor material, and cloth. The tailor supplied the work only. This man had so many current orders that when he had to grab a piece of fabric or client's package to cut it, everything would tumble off the shelves. His customers were part of the society upper crust, Jewish as well as Lithuanian. There were five of us in the workshop: the father, his two sons, a family relative, and myself. One of the sons was my age and had the same first name, and the other son was three years older. His craft became so greatly prized and the product was so sought after that the tailor had a lot of trouble keeping up with orders. To be honest, he never finished on time, and customers were forced to return several times for the same order. But in spite of it, they all wanted a new item of clothing to be made by him, and his fashion became a trend, to the point of fomenting some kind of snobbery.

The house was not as large as was needed for such an enterprise. It consisted of a large workshop and an immense bedroom as well as a smaller room that had a dual use: fitting room and waiting room in one part but also a bedroom in which the sofa served as a bed where the third child slept, a beautiful young girl for whom I harbored secret feelings. The studio was convertible, transforming into a large dining room for *shabbes* and holidays.

My last boss was a tall man who stood straight as a pillar. He was a heavy smoker whose cigarette never left his lips and had a typical constant slight cough. But above everything else, he was a good and personable man who knew a lot. It was with him that I first began to pay a little attention to my appearance. He helped me put together a small wardrobe for a young man, and I can still see myself buying the material for a suit and matching raincoat. He made me a gift of all the accessories, cut the two pieces himself, and let me use my work time to craft these elegant clothes. It tells you just how much generosity and friendship were in him. Did he think of me as an orphan who needed his support? It is obvious that he always acted like a father toward me. His benevolence was hidden behind a mask of humor and practical joking.

His only fault was a slightly excessive way of demonstrating his irony, notably at the expense of his wife. I remember these little moments like they were yesterday. He was earning a decent-enough living, but he kept the proceeds in a small purse in his pocket. When his wife came to ask him for money to go on an errand, he took out the purse and began to joke around to irritate her, to *khokhmen*, wisecracking, meaning he was trying to be witty. When his audience had all been won over, he would ask, slightly seriously at first and then inquiringly, as if there was nothing unusual, what was all this fuss about? His wife, who had patience to spare, never got angry and ended up getting all that she wanted. She was a bit chubby—let us say she was a plump woman with a house full of kids. She showed herself to be a generous character with a kind word for everyone and found a moment to devote to one and all without ever forgetting me or the other workers in the studio. She never involved herself with the work, but when we were staying late to finish an order, she served everyone the same meal. And that would happen often because for Jews the workweek is always too short, especially on Friday afternoon in winter when the *shabbes* comes too soon. Time we lost from Friday afternoon through Sunday had to be made up. We were devoted and loyal, we didn't keep track of our hours, and by working late we were able to make more money than during the day. He paid us generously. I learned all the tricks of the trade, and if I think about it, that was where I really learned women's tailoring as well as the ropes of men's tailoring and was therefore able to do better for myself and do more for my family.

What's more, I enjoyed myself so much at his house that I paid him visits on public holidays as well as Saturdays and Sundays just to spend time in his good company. Naturally, his two sons were my friends, but there were also his two girls and their girlfriends who came to visit. What can I say? A man has a heart, and a heart is not made of stone. I would soon be an adult, and at that age we are easily distracted; we dream and cherish hopes. In moments of elation, we even picture ourselves the handsomest of men, and we literally see the chance to please any girl ready to fall in love at first sight as though struck by lightning. It was, however, all fantasy, my imagination getting the best of me.

No doubt I have been dwelling too much on the tailors because what I was preoccupied with more than anything else, my personal burden, or at least my major worry, was the day-to-day feeding of my family. As soon as I found a job with good tailors, I began dressing well. I also saw to it that my brothers were decently dressed. My mother's sisters in America continued to send us packages of used—but usable—clothes for her and the youngest children, and some rare money continued to arrive from her brother in South Africa, at the same pace. With my earnings we ended up living decently, if modestly. My father, now that I think about it, continued to send letters that always contained the same refrain: as soon as he was earning more, he would arrange for all of us to come to Paris. Yosef, studying to become a teacher, began to learn French.[2] But all his promises remained a dead letter, and that never changed; my father never even took the first concrete step to start the paperwork, and we remained in Telz right up until the war.

Given the circumstances, was I happy as a young man? Since my father was still alive, I didn't have the right to call myself an orphan, but even so, I grew up feeling like one. Until the age of thirteen or fourteen, my adolescence had been profoundly troubled. But later on I cannot say I was truly unhappy, despite the fact that our material situation still weighed heavily on my shoulders, forcing me to adopt adult responsibilities at a very early age. I was barely nine when my father left, and at that age I clearly had trouble untangling the true from the false. Within a few years, however, I understood that my father left because he had been ashamed of the bankruptcy. Instead of dealing with reality and trying to save all of us, he took, probably unconsciously, the easy way out, sidestepping the ordeal and not taking us into account.

That first year passed between sorrow and hope. We were under the illusion that we would soon be united, the family, the household, and all its contents. At the very beginning, he had really seemed to plan for us to join him in Paris. But dreams do not always come true. Later, he must have concluded that it would be more convenient for him to live alone. After that, nothing looked the same. Hope

2. Telz, beside its renowned yeshiva, had numerous educational institutions. In addition to the *khederim* for boys and the four levels of *folkshul* (elementary school) classes for the girls, a *kollel* (postgraduate institute) was started in 1922 to train students for the rabbinate. In 1920 the Gymnasium Yavneh (eight grades of secondary school) for girls was established. In 1925 the Yavneh School for teacher training was created, and soon after, in 1930, a women's branch of the teacher training school opened, with a two-year course. The very high level of education, both secular and religious, offered by these two women's schools attracted not only teenagers and young women of the region but also daughters from all Lithuania and Poland who were sent by their families to Telz for its educational excellence. See http://batkamaat.org/?page_id=16.

became anger, and anger became hate. But hating a father that you miss, expecting one who is never coming back, is a very special mistrust. Only children torn between two feelings, and whose mother or father has abandoned them, can understand the spiritual and physical distress that such an absence imposes. But there will be an occasion to discuss my father again when I talk about our reunion after twenty-seven years of separation. I won't tell you that I lived all day every day with this nightmare. I spent my time like other people my age, and I was a life-loving boy. All things considered, it all depends on what an individual needs to feel satisfied. As everything in life is relative—if an individual is only gazing up at others having more and being better off, then clearly unhappiness will ensue. In spite of the adversity, I managed to be happy with what life had given me.

Of course, I spent most of my youth working hard, but I knew how to get the most from my spare time. I must have slept, but I don't know when. We always finished work between ten and midnight, when all of us, tailors, cobblers, and craftsman of whatever trade, got together to have fun well into the night. Saturday and Sunday were for us "America," the golden land, when a whole bunch of us got away from the city. As there were no buses in town, only a few taxis, and two fire trucks, before even planning any of our adventures we each had to get hold of a bicycle to travel around more freely. The rider had to be very steady not to fall on the roads cobbled with irregular stones. Out of town, of course, meant only a few minutes from the city. In whatever direction we went, we were in the country immediately.

To tell the truth, relationships with Jewish girls were next to impossible. And even if a few of them might have agreed to take pity on us, they were the girls whose beauty and style left something to be desired. The girls I coveted would never have agreed to accompany us or to be seen in town with a boy. Most of them were the daughters of proper religious families, and many attended the Yavne Gymnasium, the girls high school in Telz, which had a solid reputation. These young persons were so proud of their fine education that they deliberately spoke Hebrew among themselves on the street instead of our vernacular Yiddish. Sometimes, we would get a date with a shikse, a Christian girl; however, we paid some attention to whether she was anti-Semitic. In contrast to the Jewish girls, they had fewer principles, and let's say that they were less picky regarding boys who were less advantaged.

Other friends had a pronounced taste for politics, such as my brother Yosef, who was active in Betar, a right-wing organization.[3] You could observe them while they paraded in the park, uniformed like soldiers, holding a stick firmly in hand. Like other political parties, they had a place to hold meetings, after which they would sing and dance. I started showing up on the sly, not because I had embraced their program, but to play Ping-Pong for free. Betar also had an amateur football team, and as you already know I loved the game. Little by little, I began to play with them, until they finally co-opted me as a team member, even though I never joined their organization. It offered me the opportunity to travel with the team to other cities for matches against Jewish or Lithuanian teams. The son of my boss hung out at Betar, as did my best friend, who was also a member. As you may figure out, I would have had sufficient pretexts to get closer to Betar, but I joined no party right up until the start of the war. I don't know why; it just didn't speak to me or have any hold on me. Immediate issues of survival were perhaps more important than attending political meetings that were held during work hours.

My closest friend, whom I adored, came from a family that raised livestock; more precisely, they bought and sold horses and cows. The family lived in a wood house with two levels above the ground floor, which was considered pretty spacious for Telz. The household was filled with children. In the vast courtyard was a stable sheltering cattle over which was a barn where fodder was stored. They kept their own cows in this yard, as well as animals that remained there until they could be sold. These animals underwent a health treatment,

3. Betar, Hebrew בית״ר, also spelled Beitar, a nationalist Zionist militarized youth movement founded by Vladimir Ze'ev Jabotinsky in 1923, in Riga.

because they often needed a little care. They were given better food for a specific period of time, and when at last they regained some elegance, they were put on the market. I remember one day my friend bought an exhausted horse so weak that he was close to dying and no longer able to stand. After several weeks being coddled in improved surroundings, the nag ended up looking respectable. On the day he was brought to market in Telz, the creature had been bathed, coiffed, brushed, and gussied up like a veritable bridegroom. In those days, in order to add a little punch and allure to these poor animals, a hot potato was used as a suppository. The revived animal easily yielded triple its purchase price.

Not far from town, the family owned a farm where grass grew copiously before being cut, then dried in the open air and brought to town to be stored in the granary in anticipation of winter. Because there was no machine that could serve the purpose, we would all cut the grass by hand and, once it had been cut, fan it out for drying and gather it in small mounds that were piled onto a wagon, heaping it quite high. Climbing to the top of this grand edifice was my great reward, and the trip into town is something that has still not left me. Though I loved this family for who they were, I felt a deep attraction for the countryside that has never flagged.

My friend's mother pampered me like one of her own children. When I arrived at their house when they were having their meal, she always invited me to sit down at the table, and I am forced to admit that this was a house of good and plenty. When she was cooking up a pot, it was enough to feed an army. Other than sugar and salt, the family bought nothing in the stores because the farm produced everything: milk products, of course, butter and fresh cream, but eggs, fruits, and vegetables as well. At the time when my mother had already sold our cow, she would never let me leave without a container of milk. They ate meat every day, something rather rare in Telz, slaughtering a calf or a sheep and eating it over a certain period. They grew all kinds of vegetables and baked their own bread. My friend was a tall, solid young man, muscled by physical work. We were very attached to each other and went bathing and swimming together. He was not averse to showing his strength, and even the Lithuanian boys were scared of him. We liked going on outings on the lake in a rowboat, hooking up with other friends because the cost for just the two of us was too high. My friend offered me the opportunity to perfect my horseback riding, which was to prove very valuable during the first year of the war. In addition, we both played on the Betar football team, even though I was able to devote myself to this passion only on Sundays.

At home, my behavior had started changing. I saw myself as the head of the family, the *balebos*, and conducted myself like I was the boss, especially, I would say, with my older brother. With a definite arrogance I made him understand that I was *der broyt geber*, the one bringing home the bread every day. My little brothers were still just docile boys, and I adored them, but of Yosef I was jealous. In contrast to me, he was an intellectual and showed off, well groomed and elegant in spite of our modest means—it is how I saw it back then. Feeling the weight of my sacrifice, I considered that he too should have been able to work instead of always being on the take. More often than not, he would fly in and out of the house, and I couldn't quite figure out where he would sit himself down to study, but that didn't prevent him from being an excellent student. He was a very talented boy, according to everyone who knew him. Looking back on my feelings, I realize the derision and especially the stupidity I demonstrated. But that's the way things are when you are young: you sometimes act as if the entire world belongs to you, like an egotist, needless to say. I had immense respect for my mother and loved her more than anyone in the world. All she really needed was to feel supported, and she returned my love a hundred times over. Because I gave her everything I earned for household expenses, she was the only real boss in the house. Afterward, she would give me back some pocket money, which I was satisfied with because my needs were quite limited.

My grandfather Aaron Meyerowitz was living with us too. In those days, old people stayed at home until the final day of their lives. In spite of our economic situation, he had a room that was his alone.

As I've already said, he suffered from nose cancer, and even though he had already undergone several operations, when his nose turned gangrenous again it smelled terrible. Another operation would have been too expensive, because it would have involved several subsequent bouts of plastic surgery. The odor from his nose was becoming insufferable. Grandfather began not feeling well at night, and my mother asked me to sleep in his room, where I slept until he died. One night he fell asleep forever. I did not even hear when his breathing changed. He had lived almost one hundred years and suffered terribly from the cancer, enduring all these surgeries without a complaint. Surely, he deserved to slip away peacefully in his sleep. He was a pious man who went to synagogue three times a day for prayers, not to mention his observance of *shabbes* and holidays. He manifested, in spite of his illness, a solid appetite, which means that he was not afraid of quantities, although he expressed a most prickly disposition when it came to food. As we say in Yiddish, he wasn't a *knaper eser*, a poor eater—quite the opposite: anything he gulped down was considered *knap*, paltry, insufficient. To be more explicit, his gargantuan appetite could make him devour an entire chicken without pause or a kilo of meat with as much bread, not necessarily disdaining the potatoes and vegetables, either. And here I'm talking about an ordinary weekday meal and not a holiday celebration. When he had finished and said the blessing after ending the meal, he undertook an examination of its composition the way a critic would talk about music or film. He would say things like, "You know, Mere-Khaye," using her two first names, "I think the soup needed more salt," or "The *tsimes* [carrot dish] wasn't sweetened enough. . . . The gefilte fish needed more pepper." In this way, he would enumerate all the recent dishes, omitting nothing as he plodded through his gastronomic review. He would never do it during the meal. This was a man who was respectful! He waited until the meal was over and God had been thanked.

After he died, his room became available. I repainted it, and my mother rented it out to two lifelong spinsters from a shtetl. They were originally from the village of Luknik, near Telz. And if it's true that neither of the ladies was a prizewinning beauty or in the prime of youth (to be honest, they were long past bringing them to the nuptial canopy), the feminine presence among four boys considerably altered the atmosphere in the house. Sometimes we hugged them not too considerately or pulled their hair. Yet we have to admit the truth and not boast, because we did not dare venture beyond such teasing.

I had become a young man and had learned the modern dances. There was a dance party every week at the Lithuanian high school at a slight remove from the city, not more than five minutes away from my home. The building was brand new, and the hall for dancing, equipped with a dazzling parquet floor, was the one used as the gymnasium and also for hosting basketball games. Basketball was like a national religion that everyone venerated, as even back then the Lithuanians had a world-class team. International matches were played at night and were very well attended; most spectators were Lithuanian. I came very often to attend and went to the dances, too. Lithuanian girls came to dance as well as Jewish girls, and as long as they were willing to dance and follow the steps, I would say no to neither, because with your eyes closed the difference would simply vanish. And every Sunday, we could go dancing out of town, in the country and in the fresh air, to the sound of the accordion, which is called *gegiojina* in Lithuanian. Not a single Jewish girl ever ventured out that far.

Generally speaking, Jews in Lithuania were considered like worn pieces of inherited furniture that no one really wanted to discard. Most often, the Lithuanians manifested no animosity toward us, neither did they exhibit an excess of affection, but generally speaking our situation was not worse than in other countries. The story is told that the president of Lithuania once dropped a remark, while addressing an anti-Semitic rally, that nobody should be stupid enough to slaughter a still productive milk cow for its meat. In short, Jews had lived in Lithuania for a long time and were tolerated. In Germany the Nazis were rising, igniting anti-Semitic persecutions whose consequences very quickly invaded our doorstep. Many Jewish refugees were found wandering across Lithuania. Among them, several such families arrived in Telz, where they found temporary shelter. I want to underline here that Telz was less than sixty kilometers as the crow flies from the Prussian border. It was not long before the poisonous discourse, rife with Hitler's brand of murderous sarcasm against the Jews, infected a major portion of the Lithuanian populace. Germany was invading one country after another. The German-Soviet pact in August 1939, the agreement between Stalin and Hitler, and the division of Poland between them, with Hitler's gift of the Baltic countries to Stalin, led to the entry of Soviet armies occupying Lithuania in 1940.[4] It goes without saying, Lithuania was not strong enough to resist.

By and large, the working classes or, as they were then called, the "toiling masses," were very satisfied. At last, deliverance and freedom had come . . . The yoke and chains of exploitation were coming off. Henceforth, we would be able to organize real unions capable of defending the "working class." It goes without saying that the Communists were already in the ringside seats, their names printed boldly on the program, all levers of power tightly within the grasp of the *nomenklatura*. The wealthy and exploiters had better behave. In the streets there were music and dancing, for the Red Army did not take long in organizing concerts where their own artists performed. The Soviets really excelled at indoctrinating excited crowds.

We must honestly admit that there was no dearth of Communists of Jewish origin. In fact, they were quite numerous, as so many were workers. When the Soviet army entered, some were in jail and others were fighting underground. Did the Lithuanian and Jewish Communists think that their cause had definitively been won? In any case, they were doing their utmost to demonstrate their conviction for and loyalty to the new Communist doctrine. They began by arresting the nationalists, even garden-variety opponents. The jails were overcrowded, and the fact that the director of the Telz prison at the time was a Jew did nothing to improve relations between Jews and

4. See note 4 about the Molotov-Ribbentrop Pact in the chapter "Unter dayne vayse shtern."

Lithuanians and certainly didn't bring them closer. I was caught up in this current as though in a flood swollen by rain and melting ice. The turbulence grabbed everything in its path.

As I've said, I was not a member of any political party and wasn't even a Communist sympathizer. But my sympathies and way of thinking led me naturally to tell myself that we, working-class people, would now be better able to fight for our rights and to reject the exploitation of the bosses. As a result, my first patriotic gesture was to leave my well-loved boss and go to work in the city's only textile factory. The factory mostly made household linen from flax as well as flax fabrics for traditional suits and dresses that Lithuanians would wear on national holidays. It also made the woven fabric that was used to manufacture bags for sugar. My job was to precisely set up these bags on an enormous sewing machine. You can see how far I had progressed. From being a specialized craftsman, I had become a manufacturer of bags for sugar. To make things even better, I was earning less money than before! But the effect was to make me a more authentic proletarian who was not afraid to commit to an ideal or get my hands dirty by working.

Union involvement beckoned to me with open arms. Paradoxically, leaving my old job had freed my mind. To me, union militancy did not seem to have anything political about it. In my view, my motivations and movements were obeying a larger dynamic, the struggle for improved labor conditions and the fight over hours. Imagine what it was to go from a sixteen-hour to an eight-hour workday! We also tackled the conditions for younger apprentices with a claim for a six-hour workday. Considering what my personal story had been, once I had cut the umbilical cord to my "boss father," it was entirely natural to find myself preoccupied with such union activity and to enthusiastically throw myself into the fray. Now I had more free time than ever, since my work at the factory began at six in the morning and I was left with long afternoons. It differed drastically from when I had worked late into the night. Again and again, the union sent me to inspect the bosses to verify that workers were not working more than eight hours. It was not possible to escape the tedious task of monitoring my old bosses. Other than the first one, I had never had anything to complain about. When, at eight in the evening, I showed up at precisely the job I had just walked away from, he would look at me in silence, surprised, somehow sardonically, and with a trace of sorrow. He had not submitted to the new regulations, and after my visit he continued his usual practice, striving just as hard to make ends meet.

A partner was usually assigned to go out on these duties with me. On one such inspection I was assigned a new comrade, a young girl my brother Yosef occasionally met during his activities and knew better than I did. As it turns out, she was going to play an important role in my future. I had been to her uncle's house on occasion and had even worked for him at one time. I remember perfectly how, after our inspection, we went to my house to finish a task, the purpose of which we are to this day completely unable to remember, or what we spoke about, or how it ended. Simple coincidence or divine will, this encounter with my destiny was, at first sight, of no consequence.

This auspicious period could not last. The dream of a better life vanished on the beautiful summer morning of June 22, 1941, when the Germans assaulted the Soviet Union and war began. On the war's second day, Telz had not yet been occupied. Before they retreated, the Communists took the political prisoners, mostly members of the pro-Nazi militias, out of the jail, led them to a wooded area beyond the city in a place called Rainiai, and shot them.[5] When the Germans entered Telz less than a month later, the Nazis and Lithuanians seized on these executions as a pretext for revenge and, claiming that they were avenging their martyrs, led the Jewish men and young people to an area of fields and glades, also in Rainiai, and shot them all. The women and children were massacred in August and September. In the three months that followed, the Lithuanians and the Germans undertook to extinguish centuries of Jewish life on Lithuania's soil.

5. See http://batkamaat.org/?page_id=2212.

Cataclysm

The Germans attacked from all sides and advanced in every direction. Cities closer to the frontier would be occupied later, while those in the interior were captured by lateral and in-depth breakthroughs, having encirclement as their objective. These German tactics meant that, despite its proximity to the border, by the war's second day Telz was still unoccupied. At the factory where I worked and where I was the only Jew, I was assigned to a civil defense unit. I was provided a wagon hitched to two draft horses, strong like elephants, or, rather, as we would say in Yiddish, like lions.

Wagons served the equivalent purpose of trucks today. Expected to perform a variety of tasks, including courier, ambulance driver, and so forth, I was also taught how to rescue the injured and transport them to the hospital. As I was crisscrossing the town, on the third day of the war, I had still not seen any wounded on my rounds. Those who were able to flee had done so on the first day. We could already hear the noise of thundering cannon and of overflying planes. Because Telz had no strategic or military importance, military planes went back and forth without bombing us. But the Germans still intended to use the element of psychological warfare and terrorized the civilian population by buzzing us with their planes a few dozen meters above our heads. It felt to me that the Germans were at the very gates of the city.

Life is such that we are also driven to act on our premonitions. An unknown voice spoke to me, and an unknown hand prodded me, "Moishe, do not stay in this hellhole." My mother had taken my two younger brothers and gone just outside the city to stay with

Lithuanian peasant farmers she knew. Now I had to go at all costs with my makeshift vehicle and get her. When I found her, I told her that the wagon was our only chance to save ourselves. "Let's leave and protect ourselves by going to Russia," I said. She replied, "*Mayn kind*, I am in poor health. Where would you have me wandering? I know the Germans very well. We lived with them, shared their border as good neighbors during the world war. They are educated people. I speak their language as well as they do, and they will not do me any harm." I understood there was nothing I could do to convince her to undertake such an uncertain flight, that it was pointless to insist or argue. I hugged her and my two brothers, and I was off. Not for a moment did it occur to me that I would never see them again. If I only could have imagined their tragic end, I would have taken them with me by force and never have abandoned them to the mercies of the Germans.

My older brother, Yosef, was not with them, and I never saw him again, never had the chance to give my farewell, or say good-bye. I remain doubtful to this day of the account I heard that placed him at the Iranian frontier. The person telling me this story was from Telz and said he had spoken to him at the Iranian border, where Yosef had confided to him that he was trying to get across and make it to Palestine. I suspect this person had made up this narrative only to assuage me. Yosef surely suffered the same fate as Leybe and Eli.

I was convinced that I had to flee as fast as I could. But traveling with two horses hitched to a wagon was too risky, so I chose a bicycle as my means of transport. I had an old one in pitiful condition that would have needed serious repairs to make such a long journey. The endeavor was contingent on quick and properly considered planning. The city had emptied of its population, but I knew at whose house I could "borrow" a solid and brand-new bicycle. The house had been closed up, so I had no choice but to crawl through a window and go out the same way. I admit it wasn't a very nice thing to do, not very Christian . . . or very Jewish for that matter. Of course . . . if the person would have survived, I would have repaid him three time its price! If it's true that to save your own skin one might ignore finer

Telsa.
Riga
PSKOV
NOVGOROD
RYBINSK
KOSTROMA velo fix
NiŽNiy NoVGORod velo
   VoLGA KAZAN
MER CasPiENNE
   ASTRAKHAN
allée-retour
iEKATRiNSBURG=SVERdloVsk
KURGAN
   Perm
OMSK
   TOMSK
ALMA-ATA
TACHKENT
   KARŠi

le¹ Retour.
   Tadkent
SARATOV
   TULA
   ORLOV
BiELORUSSiE
via Lituanie
   ViLNiUS
   KOuNAS
   SiAULiAi
   TELSIIAi
(MEMEL) KLAipEdA
tiLsit-KönigsberG

TELSiai - Riga = 400 KM.
Riga - PSKoV = 300 KM
PSKoV - NoVGORod = 200 KM
NoVGORod - RyBiNSK = 400 KM
RYBiNSK - KostoRoMA = 360
                        ____
avec le velo   1600 KM.
KostoRoMA - NiŽniy NoVGorod 360 Km
              La pied.
         VoLGA
NiŽNiy - NoVGoRod = KAZAN 300 KM
           VoLGA
KAZAN - ASTRAKHN = 1000 X 2 = 2000 Km
        Allee retour.
KAZAN iEKATERiNSOURG SVERdLovsk 600 Km
SVERdLOVSK - OMSK   600 Km
OMSK — TOMSK   600 Km
TOMSK - ALMAJA   1200 Km
ALMATA - TASKENT   700 F
TASKENT - KARSi A/R 400x2
                  = 800 F
TASKENT - SARATOV 1200 Km
SARATOV - TULA   500 Km
TULA (KiNESberg) 1200 Km
 Klapeda(KALiNOGrad)
         + TiLZiT

          M600

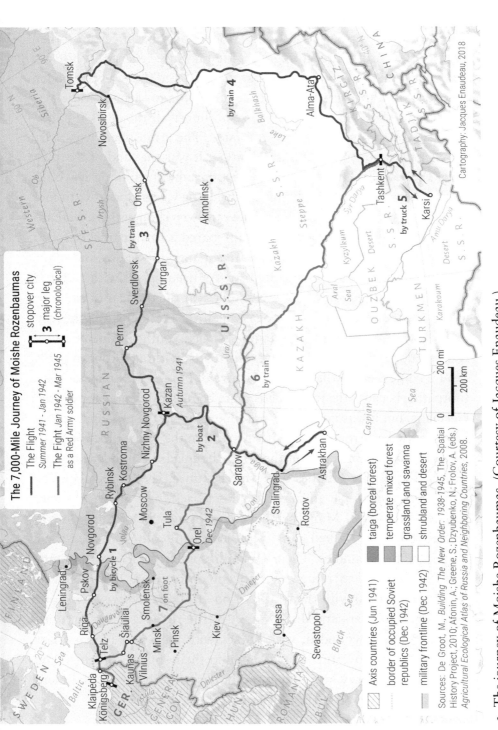

The 7,000-Mile Journey of Moishe Rozenbaumas

— The Flight
Summer 1941 - Jan 1942

○ stopover city

⊢—⊣ **3** major leg
(chronological)

— The Fight *Jan 1942 - Mar 1945*
as a Red Army soldier

taiga (boreal forest)

temperate mixed forest

grassland and savanna

shrubland and desert

Axis countries (Jun 1941)

border of occupied Soviet
republics (Dec 1942)

military frontline (Dec 1942)

Sources: De Groot, M., *Building The New Order: 1938-1945*, The Spatial
History Project, 2010; Afonin, A.; Greene, S.; Dzyubenko, N.; Frolov, A. (eds.)
Agricultural Ecological Atlas of Russia and Neighboring Countries, 2008.

Cartography: Jacques Enaudeau, 2018

2. The journey of Moishe Rozenbaumas. (Courtesy of Jacques Enaudeau.)

points of the law, then Jewish law at least provides a certain order of priorities. Before everything else, life takes precedence. While it's true that I did not believe in God at the time and didn't even ponder the question, the fact is that the bike was going to save my life.

Fearing that Telz would be seized, almost all the city's inhabitants had taken refuge in the countryside. The atmosphere was marvelous that summer, the sun unrelenting. It was the kind of weather for a vacation and not for war. I must have been thinking it would last forever, and I gave no thought to bringing warm clothes with me, not even a woolen garment or underwear. Even though there were no reserves in our house, I nevertheless prepared a small parcel of food. And so I left home in a shirt and pair of pants. I rode day and night while managing brief periods of rest. As if equipped with radar, I headed in the direction where I wouldn't hear the thunder of cannon, and along the way I would ask peasants if the Germans were nearby or far away. You can easily imagine what a youth of nineteen was feeling, alone on extremely dangerous roads, without a roof over his head. I confess easily that I was very afraid. I took back roads or even footpaths, because the main roads were being strafed nonstop by the Germans, but it was not always possible to avoid the principal routes because the back roads didn't always lead in the right direction.

What was happening on the roads boggled the mind. Everyone was fleeing. Entire families were on the move, some on wagons or by foot. Some people advanced on horseback, and many, like me, traveled by bicycle. Many perched their meager belongings on top of their bike and walked alongside them, while others nestled their bikes atop their bundles. There was no respite in the German bombing, and defenseless refugees, innocent unfortunate civilians who had nothing to do with the war, had no idea how to save their poor lives. The shoulders and ditches next to the road were strewn with corpses and the wounded, with horses with their guts blown apart by bombs, with overturned wagons and their spilled contents. The blood flowed everywhere, along the flanks of both horses and men. It was a slaughter. At night the planes attacked less.

No doubt our ordeal took on an even more colossal dimension by the Red Army fleeing along the same main roads. In its ranks, the dead numbered in the hundreds and the wounded in the thousands. The military retreat increased the chaos of the civilian exodus. Among the thousands were men and women with children in their arms, as well as the elderly who walked along with great trouble, and adding to the dread were the soldiers of the routed army and their thousands of wounded. The enemy planes were obviously aiming for the military transports loaded with munitions. Like black eagles they dove, plunging with a noise to wake the dead. The bombs rained down, and as if that weren't enough, the German planes opened fire with machine guns. Everyone ran with the sole idea of burrowing somewhere, and in the panic the cries and howls of mothers and their children were indescribable. Some of the children lost their parents and never found them again. It was an apocalyptical vision.

Rosa, who would become my wife after the war, made her escape with her family thanks to her father, Baruch, who worked as a teamster and owned a horse and wagon. He had gathered his family with some other neighbors of the courtyard they lived in and saved this little crowd from the fate otherwise in store for them. They survived in the Urals, deep inside of Russia, four thousand kilometers from Lithuania. At the outset of this mad exodus, Rosa had witnessed her maternal grandmother get off the wagon. The elderly woman had forgotten to feed the hens.[1] Nothing and no one could dissuade her. She must have reckoned that she'd already had her fill of hardships. Her family never saw her again. In order to grasp the tragedy of war, one must have watched such scenes and felt the grip of terror such situations actually etched into the human soul.

1. In Hayim Grade's novel *Zelmenyaner*, an aunt, *di mume* Hessie, also leaves a wagon for strange reasons relating to poultry while the family tries to escape the bombings and is mowed down by a cannonball. But the story takes place at the beginning of World War I.

I had gotten away from Telz by using the back roads in the direction of Latvia. Before leaving, I had prepared myself and taken care to gather up a number of maps that I scrounged up at the Lithuanian high school. I also packed some candles and some matches and got hold of a flashlight as well as a sort of metal flask for drinking water. I had visited the apartment of a Russian general that I kept on guarding long after everyone had escaped town. There I left a pistol without even touching it, not knowing what to do with it. Caught in a tough situation, I didn't overthink my choices. I made do with the circumstances and was somehow not so badly prepared for such a long and arduous journey. But when I arrived in Latvia, the foreignness felt complete, and figuring out which path to choose to avoid running into the Germans got more complicated than in Lithuania. Although Latvian is a Baltic language similar to Lithuanian, communication with the inhabitants wasn't easy. Russian, a language I spoke pretty poorly myself back then, wasn't familiar to the Latvian peasants, either. Still, I did finally make it to Riga, Latvia's capital, where the shelling was very violent. In extremis, I managed to get across the river just in time. The only bridge was bombed immediately after I reached the other side. As luck would have it, Rosa's family, who had fled three days before me, had taken the same bridge and been close enough to witness its destruction too.

From here I didn't go toward Estonia and its capital, Tallinn, but pressed on toward Russia, aiming for the city of Pskov. I was doing legs of about two hundred kilometers in a twenty-four-hour period. The biggest problem was finding a place to sleep at night for a few hours. Most of the time, I slept outside with my head cradled on top of my bicycle, not for a pillow, but because I was afraid someone would steal it. Occasionally, I found a refuge among peasants for part of the night, happy for the shelter of a cowshed or, better still, in the hay, where sleep is so sweet when one is tired.

As I penetrated deeper into Russian territory, I want to emphasize how friendly was the hospitality of the Russian peasants. They never failed to offer a piece of bread with a glass of milk. The Russian people, the peasantry especially, beyond any political consideration, have an absolutely extraordinary generosity of soul and heart. As soon as the fear of bombs had lessened, I started to catch my breath. The major problem now was feeding myself, as I had long since run out of the meager provisions I had taken from home. The first step was to sell my watch, which gave me enough for a little while.

I continued on my way to Moscow, or, to be more precise, along an axis between Moscow and Leningrad—St. Petersburg today—on my way to Novgorod. From my fear of shelling, I still passed through cities and towns as quickly as possible. The farther I got from home, the more alone I felt. My stomach was never full, I wasn't sleeping enough, and I was never clean. I had no soap and most of the time would wash in the rivers I passed on my bicycle. I would not see soap again for several long months, when I was inducted into the Russian army. From Novgorod I made it to Rybinsk, and from there to Kostroma, and then to Nizhny-Novgorod. Broken by fatigue, exhausted and famished, I had covered a very long distance. I no longer knew what day it was or how long I had been wandering the roads. I had left without a dime in my pocket and didn't have a change of shirt or underwear. I was wearing everything I owned. I had no roof over my head but decided to call a halt and rest for a while. Also, the bicycle had become a burden because I had to continually keep an eye on it so it wouldn't be stolen out from under me. I decided to sell it, which thankfully posed no problem. In those days, you could buy and sell anything. With the money I got for it I was able to get enough to eat for a while. Although I obtained a good price, bread and produce were unreasonably expensive. Even an onion cost a fortune. When one lacks food, vitamin deficiencies are not long in coming, and teeth start to loosen and fall out. In a situation of extreme want, a piece of bread and an onion were nothing less than a luxury.

I was not alone in this predicament; thousands of people were in the same situation, arriving from everywhere along the different raging fronts of the war. Everyone was running in the same direction, away from the fighting. Refugees were sleeping in public buildings, but mostly in the streets. The authorities had opened every place with available space. I ended up meeting an acquaintance, a young man from Plunge, a town close to Telz. I used to go to Plunge fairly often to visit relatives, my mother's cousins, the Zalkanovitch family. They had two boys and a girl who were all Lithuanian high school students. The parents were very friendly people, and every time I visited they expressed a generous hospitality and received me so open-heartedly, as though I was one of their own children. It is worth underlining that this whole family survived the Shoah, an extremely rare occurrence for Lithuanian Jewish families. The parents died after the war. Their daughter and one son immigrated to Israel with their families. The other son remained in Plunge with his family, but he is gone now. Are there any Jews left in Plunge today?

I knew the young man from frequently playing for the Betar football team from Telz in games against his team, the Hapoel,[2] the workers of Plunge, where he used to play opposite me. He was a blacksmith by trade, not at all a Jewish career, but in the very small city of Plunge, located in a rural area with a large peasant population, he was sitting on a gold mine. As a result, the blacksmith really had it made and commanded all the clientele he could have desired. He made the horseshoes in his workshop and shod the horses himself. He also made iron rims for wagon wheels that were still being made of wood. Big and strong with the large callused hands of a manual laborer, he was three years older than I was. Even though we had never been the closest of comrades, when I met up with him it was like I had found a member of my family. There had not been a single person to exchange a word with along the entire length of the journey. I had been so forlorn that he came as a godsend, and I think he felt the same way. Shouldering a potato sack this time, I set off in his company. Our goal was to make a tour of the nearby *kolkhoze*, the collective farms of the Soviet regime.

---

2. Hapoel הפועל, Hebrew, literally "the worker," sport association. It was established in 1926 as a union of the Histadrut, in Palestine, and represented the workers' class.

In the USSR, where land had been confiscated from the peasants—many of whom had been deported—the *kolkhoze* represented the state-owned units of production that had perpetual title
to the land and collective ownership of the means of production.
Everyone worked together and at the end of the year received his
share of the produce along with a little money. In addition to their
respective dwellings, everyone had a small plot of land that they
could cultivate for their own needs. Why were we going to the *kolkhozes*? Because we knew there was a shortage of male workers,
especially blacksmiths. The men had been drafted into the army,
and the only ones left were the elderly, women, and children. My
friend did the forging, and I looked after the fire, working the bel-
lows and striking the anvil with the big hammer. In exchange for
the work we furnished, the residents provided us something to eat,
a place for the night, and a little money. Working like this, we saved
bread to build up a small reserve. It was very black bread with not
a little bit of straw mixed in with the flour. It kept for about two
weeks and then became very hard, but our teeth were still good
enough. And so we wandered from one *kolkhoze* to another until
we arrived in Kazan.

Kazan is a port on the Volga whose population contains a large
Tatar majority, descendants of the people who had wreaked havoc
among the Russian people in the sixteenth century, particularly in
the Crimea but also in other regions of Greater Russia.[3] They were
neither very warm nor very friendly. In an absolute sense, of course,
there are no bad, wicked, or bellicose people, and all such general-
izations are abusive and hurtful. But given our circumstance, it was
totally the impression we had. It was hard to have a conversation
with them because not everyone spoke Russian, and those who did
had no wish to speak to us, owing to their hostility toward Russians.

3. The Crimean Tatars attacked Russia in 1507, followed by two centuries
of Russo-Crimean wars for the Volga basin. These wars ended with the Russian
conquest of the Kazan khanate.

The city was built on the Volga, Europe's longest river, coursing more than 3,700 kilometers and emptying into the Caspian Sea via a large delta. During the war, the Volga was of inestimable strategic importance, as it is the major navigable artery that connects the White Sea to the Baltic via the Volga-Baltic Canal as well as the Aral Sea to the Black Sea via the Volga-Don Canal. It is so wide in places that you cannot see to the opposite bank with the naked eye. In bygone days, the peasants under serfdom, the muzhiks, hauling the boats were singing the legendary song of the Volga boatmen, "*Ej Uhnem*! Эй, ухнем" (Yo, Heave Ho!). The boats now had motors, but there was no lack of any kind of craft imaginable, including dinghies and small barges that the farmers and fishermen powered by oars. All around, nature's cover of grove and forest was absolutely splendid. The timber was exploited for construction and furniture as well as paper manufacturing. Trees were cut on the heights, and the trunks were then slid downhill into the river and there, attached one to another, forming kinds of rafts that peasants and fishermen powered by oars to the Caspian Sea. Kazan is a harbor city and was equipped with all the installations necessary to load and unload passengers and freight arriving from and departing to every conceivable destination. During the war, the port bubbled like a pot. We observed merchandise going out toward the battlefield—the goods were, of course, essentially reserved for the military—as the returning transports brought back the gravely wounded.

I am describing that as if we were already on board. On a beautiful morning we climbed aboard a freighter going down to the Caspian Sea, but not so quickly and not so simply. The trip took several days. Taking advantage of each stopover, we disembarked at every port, walked around town, and then boarded another boat. Why were we wandering around like this, and what were we looking for? To tell the truth, we didn't know. For sure, if we may have looked like tourists, we were not. Neither of us knew what to do or where to go. One port followed another, leaving one vessel to get on board the next—I can't remember the name of all the towns we docked at before arriving finally at Astrakhan, where we didn't stay very long either. We boarded another freighter (we usually took freighters because it was easier to find space), going back up the river this time without stopovers to Kazan. We still had a little bit of our bread and money remaining. When disembarking in Kazan, the crush of people was incredible because here, like everywhere in Russia, these trips were free. We weren't thinking about keeping our eyes open and guarding our "treasure," and too late did we realize our meager capital had been stolen. We had made it a habit of sharing what we had and hiding it on our persons, but you have to understand what novices we were. What else did the thieves find in our pockets other than the holes? Probably not a lot, but whatever it was, the small bills and the few coins would have come in very handy to buy a vegetable to go with our bread. Fortunately, there was still some bread left, which kept us from starving to death.

We had the good sense, and were clear-headed enough, to look around and notice that summer was coming to an end and the leaves were beginning to fall. Autumn in Russia comes pretty early, and we were dressed very lightly in shirts that were in tatters from being washed. After thinking about it, we realized that the simplest thing to do was to go toward where the sun was hot year-round. For transportation this time we chose a train. The trains were literally packed: people were piled on top of one another. And the odor, it simply gagged you; a gas mask would not have been amiss. No one had a sleeping cabin, and only some few people found places to sit, not even on the floorboards. Our destination was Tashkent, capital city of the Republic of Uzbekistan, near Iran and Afghanistan, very close to China. As anyone can observe on a map, we still had a few thousand kilometers to travel. After a wait that seemed very long, the train got under way. It crawled along so slowly, stretching out at such a length, bending along the curves, that it was impossible to catch sight of the front. Only after we had traveled the first few kilometers did we think about beginning to search for a little corner where we could settle ourselves, even if it was in the corridor. The train continued to move along as fast as a slug and stopped for a long time at every station. We would get off and look for the *kipyatok*, the traditional boiling water that was available everywhere to make tea or coffee and that mothers used to prepare their babies' bottles.[4] To us it brought immense relief and warmed our bellies. We also used these stops to wash up with cold water.

The trip dragged on endlessly because railways were interrupted for the slightest reason. No one was in a position to understand the mysteries of this chaotic advance. Sometimes, in open country, like a small local train stopping at every cowshed, we were remaining immobile for hours, in the middle of nowhere. One could rationalize all this by explaining it away as the priority given to military transports. Train travel was no walk in the park. Not only were we clueless about the reasons a given train would start rolling in slow motion, and on the spur of the moment, but we also didn't know with any certainty where it was going. We climbed aboard a car with the hope that the convoy was going in the right direction and were perfectly happy if the train just seemed ready to set off and not remain stuck in place. There was no shortage of trains traveling in every conceivable direction, however, so no one could say for sure where they were going or even less when they would arrive. Sometimes a few military cars would be coupled to a civilian train and then head toward some unforeseen destination where the cars would be uncoupled.

From Kazan we took the direction of the Ural. It is more accurate and based in reality to say that we were headed toward the Ural Mountains, given the transportation hazards. Approaching the mountains, we soon understood that something was wrong regarding our destination. We chose this moment to simply leave the train for a round of visits to the *kolkhozes*, to replenish our supply of bread and to eke out a small wage. A funny habit this compulsion to eat every day. It sure is a strong one. We hit the road on foot with burlap potato sacks for shoulder bags. We wandered up to the outskirts of

---

4. Кипяток, *kipiatok*, Russian word for boiling water.

the city of Perm. I don't remember the names of all the towns and cities we passed anymore, but we were certainly beyond Sverdlovsk, now called Yekaterinburg. We came in sight of a village that from a distance had us thinking we were looking at a *kolkhoze*. It is how it appeared from afar, but when we got nearer and noticed soldiers of the NKVD (the People's Commissariat for Internal Affairs), we realized something was amiss and turned right around. We made off in the direction our gaze carried us. Our legs followed. At the time, of course, we knew nothing about political gulags. We imagined the barbed wire was for holding nonpolitical prisoners, just common criminals, but even so we sensed that hanging around wasn't a good idea. On our way once more, our only option was to climb back aboard the Perm train for Sverdlovsk. This was the capital city of the Urals and not a bad place at all. A lot of Jews were living there, but even so we were unable to find any shelter or to rest our heads, not even for a night; we were far from being the only refugees gathering in the city. We wandered around town several days but had to resolve to get back on the road. Climbing aboard a train was no longer a problem for us; we became used to it. A packed car didn't frighten us, so accustomed had we become to wedging ourselves in and traveling in any situation, even if we had to push and shove, just like you see in a Parisian metro at rush hour. Once inside the car we always found a little nook that was sufficient to sit down, most of the time on the floor. It was enough to make us glad.

We arrived at Kurgan, where we got off the train. It was a medium-size city that held no interest for us, so we boarded a train once again. But this time it was the wrong one. We quickly realized we were going the opposite way and obviously heading into the cold instead of toward the warmth and sun. We had to react quickly, because with what we were wearing, the consequences could be catastrophic. We were scared stiff of finding ourselves in Siberia and were edging its confines. We came to Omsk first and then got to Tomsk. There was no one who could help us, and what was more, the search to find any Jewish community organization was totally futile. There hardly were any Jews in that corner of the world, but after asking around, we were advised to try our luck in Alma-Ata. The choice of transportation wasn't any different, but from there the trains going in the desired direction were rare. It seems impossible to enumerate the endless number of cities we had to pass through before finally arriving in Alma-Ata.

After all the hardship we had endured on our way to Siberia shivering from the cold, and in spite of all our other difficulties, we were still much better off compared with other travelers. We were as free as birds, with no suitcase, no backpack, and no money to guard. All we had were our two potato sacks, which, like our bellies, were half to three-quarters empty. And that was the reason we easily managed to worm our way through, jostling and climbing the few steps into the railway car when we weren't sliding ourselves in through a window. Such nimbleness was obviously beyond the reach of encumbered travelers, who had left home with their families, young children in arms, and carrying not only their luggage but also packages and bundles wrapped in sheets, which all together took up a lot of space.

We were now a long way from Tomsk—but instead of going toward Tashkent, which was our original destination and where all the refugees were flooding into, we were heading farther east, toward China's western border, along the southern confines of Russia. When we arrived at Alma-Ata, it was indeed warm and beautiful, and this was a crucial factor in our survival. Suffering with hunger is less painful when you are warm, as the cold weather intensifies your misery.

I was a young man from a town of eight thousand souls, and I'd never been farther from home than Kaunas, which had been the capital of Lithuania between the two world wars, two hundred kilometers away from Telz. I now found myself almost alone, thousands of kilometers from home, practically as close to China as Telz was to Kaunas. We did not attempt to cross the border because we had no say in the matter anyway. We were not masters of our fate, and the Russians would not have let us go. Our few days in Alma-Ata were not exactly merry ones. There was nothing left to eat, and we were very hungry. The people also showed themselves to be very inhospitable. The Kirghize did not even wish to use Russian. The town council fed the refugees once a day, but at Alma-Ata we learned that in the Uzbek capital of Tashkent a local committee provided for refugees. So we once again found ourselves on the train. A simple glance at an atlas will give you an idea of the many useless detours we had made since Sverdlovsk. The reality was such that we were totally reliant on the military administration.

Tashkent was truly a beautiful city, quite large and, for wartime, nearly picturesque. The sun was broiling and the heat so intense and stifling that staring at the asphalt, one would see waves in a shimmering sea. The city was indeed clean. The buildings were freshly painted, mostly white, and abundant trees and gardens gave an impression of cleanliness to this sprawling city. Swarms of people were in the streets. Refugees lay on the ground, sleeping on the sidewalks, where they cooked their food under very precarious sanitary conditions. Thousands of refugees had been evacuated by the authorities from territory occupied by the Germans, and the street provided their only free alternative, because space in public buildings requisitioned for refugees had long since been taken. Each of us had to register with the government. Once we were on the rolls, we received a ration card from an official agency. The authorities then grouped us by nationality to send us off to the villages and *kolkhozes*.

Uzbek Hell

All together we were thirteen Lithuanians, eleven young men and two women, half of whom were not Jewish. The two girls were not, and two of the men were from Riteve, a village near Telz. We didn't really like this number of thirteen, but what could we do? Some officials put us aboard a dilapidated truck with no benches to sit on, and the truck pulled out. The roads in the steppes were not asphalt or pavement but parched, dusty, hard earth, full of bumps and holes. The truck had no shock absorbers, so each bump meant we were thrown nearly twenty centimeters into the air. We drove past a lot of pastureland with hundreds of grazing sheep. In the fields, peasants planted cotton and red peppers. The route was long, and we were exhausted by hunger and fatigue. We were fed just enough to not die. My God, on what road were they taking us? For better or worse, they were driving us on the road of our destiny, and once again it was a destiny over which we were not the masters. What else can you say? It was cold at sunrise, and during the day it was scorching. The night brought an icy wind. The bumpy roads were bone-breaking. In a few days we had gone four hundred kilometers from Tashkent and were now a very short distance from the Afghanistan frontier. The closest city was Karshi (or Qarshi). They dropped us off at a cotton plantation in the middle of the steppe, in the middle of nowhere.

None of the buildings were of solid construction; only a few wooden barracks were scattered around. There was a refectory for the Uzbeks working on the plantation fields who took their midday meal for free along with shepherds from the surrounding area. It was strictly reserved for them, and we were not allowed near it. We were assigned one of these wood huts and thrown together, all piled on top of each other. We slept in a single bed or at least a sort of platform that took the place of a bed. In a corner of this one-room barrack they had placed this wooden podium, like one used by artists. But we were neither artists nor spectators but victims of war, and we were sleeping right on wooden planks. The ground was bare, packed earth, and there were no toilets or running water. With a bucket they had given us we had to walk hundreds of meters to find water. Because there was no tank or other container, we couldn't store any water, so we could just keep a minimum for drinking and for personal use. We washed near the well without any soap or towels, let alone a change of underwear. We did put some water aside for the midday meal, the only one we ate all day. You may not believe me or you may be quite skeptical, but what we were given to eat was 400 grams (14 ounces) of a very poor-quality, dark-colored flour that had not been cleaned, with the usual pieces of straw mixed in. Per person, per day, that is all that we got from our jailers, and with this we were expected to work. Making bread from it was impossible, so the only thing we could do was cook up a soup, a sort of bouillon to which we added as much red pepper as we could gather from the fields. No one could stick to this diet and be sustained very long by such a meager daily portion. We may have been young and strong— our median age was between eighteen and twenty—but none of us had eaten his fill for weeks, and our bodies were rapidly degrading. Our state of extreme deprivation and physical exhaustion had even banished any ideas about getting sexually intimate.

We were forced to leave for work on the plantation every day. Men and women were subjected to the same regimen. Our toil consisted of compacting the cotton into rectangular bales. When tied, each bale weighed about 50 kilograms (110 pounds). We lifted the load onto our backs, fitted with a special apparatus composed of a sort of belt and a board at the bottom, keeping the bale in place. When that was done, we had to transport everything to the storage facility, where there was a pyramid of cotton whose height increased as more bales were added to the pile. To reach the top we had to crawl along a plank that towered more than ten meters above the ground. The first few steps were the easiest, but climbing onto this fairly narrow board was ever more dangerous as the pyramid got higher and our heads felt wracked by hunger. Even given our young age, how long would we be able to endure such exhausting labor? The workday began at seven in the morning and was interrupted at the midday mealtime, when the Uzbeks would stop work and go to eat in their canteen, while we directed our steps to our cabin to prepare the day's only meal, the infamous soup that was prepared quickly and swallowed even quicker. It may sound strange today, but when we had finished we would approach the canteen to watch the Uzbeks eat, the saliva literally dripping from our mouths.

Cut off from the world and broken by hunger and fatigue, we didn't give a minute's thought to rebelling. With greater perspective, I can imagine how this situation might seem ridiculous, like a comical or grotesque farce, but the absolute lack of any say over the conditions that had been imposed on us played a part in this, because other than starving us and brutalizing us as slaves, the Uzbeks didn't use any violent coercion against us. The months of wandering and underfeeding, the ragged state to which we had been reduced by the thousands of kilometers we had traveled, and above all the extreme isolation in which the brutal separation from our families and homes had left us contributed to rendering our material and spiritual condition absolutely tragic. Amid the contempt and ignorance the Uzbeks displayed toward us in the middle of this actual and figurative desert, only our camaraderie allowed us to survive and to see each other as human beings.

You could never say the Uzbeks didn't have enough to eat. Quite the contrary, they had enough to burst. But they ignored us, acting like they didn't see us, because evidently they lacked the courage to look into our starving eyes. It's not easy to comprehend why they behaved this way, for sure not because we were Jews or Lithuanians. Here, like in the other Soviet republics we had passed through, hatred for the Russians ran deep, and we were probably paying the price. The Uzbeks were Muslim, did not work on Friday, and on that occasion would slaughter several sheep that were then roasted whole for several hours on spits. In a huge pot, great quantities of rice and vegetables were prepared. When everything was cooked, they assembled in the cotton field and shared their food, sitting cross-legged on the ground. Taking a fistful of rice in their left hand whose hollow also served as a dish, they used their right hand to bring the food to their mouths. To clean themselves when they had finished, they licked their fingers. Any fat that remained from the meal was soon put to good use shining the leather of their boots, handmade locally, which were incredibly supple and hardly had a sole. Imagine the despair that was ours when we took all this in. Here we were, worn out and starving, our clothes in rags and our underwear in tatters, underwear that we had been wearing since we had left our homes, and never even had a possibility to change. It was white when we left but had not resisted the weekly soapless washing and had turned brown. I don't wish a similar situation on anyone.

As terrifying as my bicycle trip had been, it had brought me into an encounter with a welcoming, cordial, and hospitable Russian people who expressed their compassion by offering a piece of bread or a glass of milk, or even a meal and a place to sleep. Compared to the Uzbeks, they were extraordinary in their kindness. Just as we refer to *la France profonde*, there is a rustic real Russia where it didn't matter whether we were Jewish or Lithuanian. They helped us simply because we were suffering human beings and needed their help. They would have given up their last piece of bread without batting an eyelash. My subsequent experience in the Russian army completely confirmed this impression, but we'll get to that a bit later on.

The labor felt more and more oppressive. When we climbed up on the plank, loaded down with our heavy cotton bales, we were seized by dizzy spells. *Khlopka* is the Russian word for cotton, but it actually also means a state of vertigo accompanied by such weakness that the legs begin to shake like chicken's feet. It had to happen, finally did happen, to each one of us. One day it was my turn to fall off the plank, followed by another comrade, who collapsed. One of us came down with typhus, and soon enough the rest of our group was contaminated. We were so weak that any illness could attack us. Abscesses began to form on our bodies and grew until they were the size of an apple. When they burst open, fountains of pus would run out.

Comatose, with high fevers, we were transported to the "hospital," if the one-story plank barrack where all the patients were lined up in a single fifty-bed room can be described this way. The room was packed. We were brought there during the phase of acute fever accompanying the typhus that lasted for two weeks while we lay unconscious. During this time you are more dead than alive. A lot of Uzbeks whom we had contaminated arrived together with us, so the hospital was crammed. When the fever finally broke, we awoke to a ferocious appetite. We had completely lost any notion of eating or even of nourishment. Rousing from our state, the sensation of being in real beds with white sheets and the sight of doctors and nurses in white blouses made us think we were dreaming. We had been brought to a palace where we were fed like sick men and not like princes. Our stomachs quickly got used to a full meal, but patient rations were insufficient, so we were now always hungry again. It's how we felt that we were slowly regaining our strength. At every bedside was a small cupboard for supplies and personal items. Obviously, because we had neither, ours were empty. The Uzbeks had clothes and reserves of food in them because their families brought in abundant food and drink. To their sick ones they gave up their best victuals, which at least speaks in their favor. As proof that our vigor was being restored little by little, we managed to organize an all-out raid on the Uzbek cupboards. The patients were still in the postcrisis period of the epidemic and almost comatose. So while everyone lay prostrate, we covered ourselves in the white sheets we slept in, and in this strange disguise we ensured our untamed restocking. In the morning the inevitable clues were discovered and a scandal erupted, but go and try to get the food of a coveted extra portion out of the stomach of a starving man. The authorities found no better solution than to padlock the cupboards. In no time at all we parried their move by learning how to pick the locks. Our return to humane living conditions had made us more clever, and the hospital had rendered us all equal, connected by a common illness. We ate thanks to Uzbek prosperity, and we were restoring our health. We can only thank them again and ask their forgiveness. Here again we touch on a moral question, and I'm the first to acknowledge it. Well, go and argue about delicate ethical questions with a stomach that is tortured by hunger and a sick body when nothing less than the survival instinct is speaking. Or one can acknowledge that the Uzbeks owed us fair reparations, after the savage treatment they had inflicted on us while we were weak and dejected, cut off from the rest of the world. You can discuss such questions for eternity, write volumes, and never arrive at a conclusion. What I do know is that we survived and saved our skins.

Once we were cured we had only one wish, which was to go back to Tashkent and enlist in the Soviet army. To our surprise, the Uzbeks needed no coaxing. On the contrary, they manifested a certain relief and seemed happy to get rid of us. They had evidently tormented us enough, and they brought us back to Tashkent in the same awful truck that we arrived in. With tears in our eyes, we appeared before the military commander and begged to be inducted. Try to imagine this proud delegation offering its military assistance to the Red Army! Dressed like bums as we were with our same rags, we had not shaved or had a haircut since the war started, we were disheveled and weakened, and, despite our recent and quick recovery after the typhus, our physical shape was not especially brilliant. They were clearly a little panicked by us and must have thought that if this was the Lithuanian contingent, then winning the war would be a long haul. They eyed us up and down and from every angle, ended up taking pity on us, and finally drafted us in the 16th Division that had been formed in 1941.[1] The two young women were also inducted

---

1. This 16th Division was first wiped out in July 1941, as Lithuanians massively deserted, joined the anti-Soviet "June Uprising," or surrendered to the Germans. Re-formed and given the title "Lithuanian," the division participated in

into the division. The case was concluded: we were fit for service. That's how we became soldiers, after having been for months refugees, then beggars, and ending up as forced labor.

---

several battles against Nazi Germany, including in Kursk, Belarus, and the Baltic. The division counted a significant number of Jewish soldiers and officers. The division disbanded in 1956. See Dov Levin, *Fighting Back: Lithuanian Jewry's Armed Resistance to the Nazis, 1941–1945*, trans. Moshe Kohn and Dina Cohen (New York: Holmes & Meier, 1985). See also Harriet Murav and Gennady Estraikh, *Soviet Jews in World War II: Fighting, Witnessing, Remembering* (Brighton, MA: Academic Studies Press, 2014).

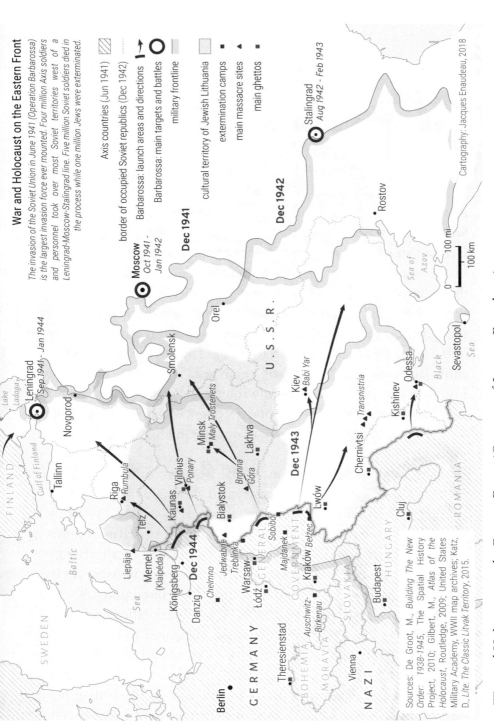

War and Holocaust on the Eastern Front

The invasion of the Soviet Union in June 1941 (Operation Barbarossa) is the largest invasion force ever mounted. Four million Axis soldiers and personnel took over most Soviet territories west of a Leningrad-Moscow-Stalingrad line. Five million Soviet soldiers died in the process while one million Jews were exterminated.

Axis countries (Jun 1941)

border of occupied Soviet republics (Dec 1942)

Barbarossa: launch areas and directions

Barbarossa: main targets and battles

military frontline

cultural territory of Jewish Lithuania

extermination camps

main massacre sites

main ghettos

Cartography: Jacques Enaudeau, 2018

Sources: De Groot, M., *Building The New Order: 1938-1945*, The Spatial History Project, 2010; Gilbert, M., *Atlas of the Holocaust*, Routledge, 2009; United States Military Academy, WWII map archives; Katz, D., Lite, *The Classic Litvak Territory*, 2015.

3. War and Holocaust on the Eastern Front. (Courtesy of Jacques Enaudeau.)

Under the Star of the Red Army

At the time of our enlistment early in 1942, the predicament of the Soviet army was disastrous. We now know that right up until the German attack, Stalin had not wanted to believe there would be war. In the years prior, the purges he had conducted into the heart of the high command had destabilized the leadership and deprived the army of its best strategists. No one had foreseen the speed and fearsome efficiency of the German offensive, which forced the Red Army into a total rout right through to 1943. The front sagged along its entire length and did not form up again until it was close to Moscow. Just as in the time of Napoléon, winter was Russia's most powerful ally, but the army's state of unpreparedness was to create a tragedy of shattering historical proportions for the military, and even more so for civilians.

Without delay, they sent us to the front within the Lithuanian military division, which had been created at the end of 1941. At present dressed up in military uniform, we were impressed by our own looks. Before we marched off, they brought us to a Russian steam bath, cut our hair, and shaved our beards. But best of all, they gave us clean underwear! It is hard to imagine how much we were cheered by our transformation. We had been given back our dignity. We were eating three meals a day now, and though military rations were nothing luxurious, the food was substantial compared to the miserable fare we had been eating. The metamorphosis spread from our bodies to our spirits. A new life was beginning . . . and if it called for sacrifice, we far preferred dying with honor on the field of battle than being starved and weakened. We could feel that we had become actual human beings again. Thanks to our rehabilitation, the turnaround in our morale was astonishing. Men could be turned into desensitized beings, into an animal form of life, made to suffer, placed in the most intolerable situations, beaten and starved, damaged beyond all moral bearing, all dignity crippled. At that point, the head is reduced to a shell, and his tormentor may continue his mistreatment; there is nothing left but a wall, because past that point, the victim greets further abuse by his persecutor with a sort of absence. Once the victim has lost all bearings, habitual and customary thought also disappears; something in the human being shuts down and reacts— in a form of mute resistance opposing the dreadful conditions I've described—with a set of survival mechanisms independent of his or her will and working almost unconsciously. In order to reverse this downfall, for dignity and pride to return, it is enough to provide a person with food and regular hygiene. Yet we knew nothing at that time of the wide-scale destruction and dehumanization the Nazis had devised in their concentration camps.

Our train came to a halt every other day, and we would be taken to the steam baths. These were a real institution that could be found in every isolated corner of the Russian territory. Steam is diffused from a structure of stones heated to white. A wooden platform allowed you to climb to the top levels where the heat becomes more intense. You were sitting there until the sweat was pouring off you. From time to time, cold water would be thrown on the stones to produce more steam, to clear the air and make it more breathable. For us, it was a real relief, helping our abscesses to heal and our strength to return little by little.

Our return trip was undeniably shorter than the one we had taken to get there, as military trains took priority over all other convoys. Leaving from Tashkent, we first headed toward the Aral Sea— and not to Siberia this time—and finally on to Saratov. After several stops, we had arrived. The 16th Division was stationed not far from Moscow, near Tula, at Yasnaya Poliana, where Leo Tolstoy's home is located. We underwent military training there before being sent to join the 249th Infantry Regiment around Orel at the beginning of

1942.[1] A foot soldier is what I became, with a rifle and a bayonet for hand-to-hand combat. That winter was very harsh, and spending the winter in the army meant living outside. We had come from a country with oppressive heat and now found ourselves in temperatures of minus thirty degrees Celsius with snow up to our knees. Fortunately, Russian soldiers were warmly clothed. We wore the *koufaike*, a top-stitched vest with a thick cotton lining, same for our pants, and under our coat the *shinel*. Naturally, we had a *shapka* on our heads, a fur cap, and on our feet the *valenki*, felt boots made of a single seamless piece of wool a centimeter thick, reaching to our knees. They did not serve as galoshes and were warm enough only in the dead of winter when it was dry and cold, but during spring and fall days, when the snow melted, they would get sodden. Unless you had been lucky enough to have found a place to dry them in the meantime, at night they would freeze into icy blocks. Instead of socks, the Russian army supplied *partianki*, rectangular bands of flannel, which we learned to wind around our feet. The unlucky ones, who did not wind them properly and had to march fifty kilometers, arrived with feet caked in blood.

The front was near Moscow and didn't move. We went into battle with our whole division. The Germans would attack, and then we would counterattack in turn. The scenario repeated itself over and over, right up to the time the Germans were halted and could advance no farther. We suffered heavy losses during our offensives, the dead and wounded numbering in the thousands. The dead were everywhere among us, frozen like blocks of ice and used as shields when we fired on the enemy. The bullets could not penetrate the corpses. The dead, German and ours, were all mixed up. Making war in snow and cold that surrounded us at all times was no easy

---

1. The Yiddish manuscript and recording had "the beginning of 1942"; the French translation has "the end of 1942," which might be a change made by Moishe while we were editing the French version.

thing. All the motorized and engineering units had the most trouble moving. Only horses hitched to sleds could advance more or less easily, and even the horses would sink up to their bellies into the snow, from which we had to help to pull them out. It happened often that the infantry advanced fifty kilometers while resupply units providing not only our food but also munitions remained stuck in the snow for several days before being able to reach the front line of the infantry. We had to deal with the shortages and wait for the logistics corps to extricate itself from the snow. Logically, the artillery was supposed to advance with the infantry, but in fact it was more a question of pushing it here and dragging it there. Toward the end, even shells were in short supply.

Trapped in the same conditions, the Germans went through more than we did. First of all, they were far from their bases. They also suffered the consequences of being at such considerable distance from their homeland. Cold was their greatest calamity and weakened them much more than it did us. Their army didn't have horses and sleds available in sufficient number to deal with the snow cover of a Russian winter. In truth they were too modern and their movements too dependent on motorized units. Their clothes weren't warm enough for our winter. They were bereft of fur hats and wearing summer caps totally inadequate for the sharp winter cold, which they tried to improve upon by adding earmuffs that looked like radio earphones. Below a certain temperature, the feet and the head have to be completely covered. The Germans had come up with funny-looking inventions to improve their caps, but all were grotesque and ended up leaving the soldier more vulnerable. Similarly, their coats and shoes were not warm enough. Shivering from head to toe, it is challenging for a soldier to become a war hero. In summer, conversely, they refused to accept defeat, held their heads high, and took advantage of their mechanized armies. Displaying a wealth of intelligence and competence, they were able to benefit from their technical superiority. One has to admit that they were excellent fighters and that their morale remained incredibly high as long as they were advancing. But after their defeat at Stalingrad in 1943, their spirits began to sag and their aggressiveness diminished, which is how things went until the end of the war.

Our division was defending a Moscow under siege. We were incorporated into the 48th Army, commanded by General Konstantin Rokossovsky.[2] After the siege of Moscow was lifted, we went on the offensive and moved in the direction of Belarus, and from there moved on toward Lithuania and the cities of Vilnius, Kaunas on the Niemen, Siauliai, the area around Telsiai (Telz, the city of my youth), and Klaipeda on the Baltic Sea, where I was born and which was annexed by Lithuania in 1923. From there we headed toward Germany, toward Tilsit, then Königsberg (Kaliningrad). This list retraces what was for us a slow progression lasting almost three years, through countless difficulties and much suffering. We were no longer getting enough to eat, didn't sleep enough or when we needed to, to say nothing of the relentless cold. Above all, there were the innumerable dead and wounded. The tears that poured from mothers and wives could fill rivers and lakes. Many of my close friends and acquaintances, among them good old friends from Telz, were not lucky enough to see the war end. The two countrymen from

---

2. Konstantin Rokossovsky (1896–1968), among the commanders of World War II, is a legendary figure of the Red Army. Arrested during Stalin's purges of the army, tortured, and put on trial, he saved his life by refusing to sign a false statement and proving to the court his NKVD accuser had been killed in the 1920 civil war.

Independent minded and a skilled strategist, he is credited with slowing down the German attack and holding the Yartsevo corridor (in the Smolensk district) open, long enough to prevent the capture and destruction of a notable part of the Soviet troops. He repeatedly resisted Stalin's obsession with counterattack described by Moishe in the following pages. Not only had he successfully implemented Mikhail Tukhashevsky's theory of "deep operation" during the Red Army counteroffensive after the turn of the Stalingrad victory, but he also led the 1944 Operation Bagration on two breakthrough fronts against the advice of Stalin. To this day, children of veterans of his army fraternize when learning of their fathers' camaraderie under his command.

Rieteve who had enlisted with me in Tashkent survived and started families in Israel.

Countless films and images of the war we have all seen show either too much or too little and are always only an approximation. The many books that have been written leave anyone who has traveled the long road of an endless war feeling perplexed. No war, of course, resembles another. And probably no experience can be compared to another. Whatever those who have been in combat may claim, there is a mortal fear for one's life that is carried in the self and is very real, which no one wants to reveal in front of their comrades. Some soldiers could not take it. They suffered nervous breakdowns, while others deserted the battlefield. It is usually not talked about much, but it is the reality of every army in the world.

The first offensives that were launched that winter in late 1942, without planning or artillery cover, were doomed to fail. We were made to run across open territory, shouting "hurrah," while well-positioned German forces fired at us as though we were rabbits. They opened fire with artillery, rocket launchers, flamethrowers, and machine guns whose powerful bullets exploded in one's body. On the battlefield, hundreds and thousands were dead, and even more were wounded, and unfortunately we could not always come to their aid. In the end, we had to fight in retreat again and again with significant losses. Not satisfied with our ways of combat and our results, the General Command sent down a new *zakaz*, an order enjoining us to start over. To comply, we reassembled the survivors and went back into battle, with exactly the same outcome. Our agony and physical misery had to be endured until the end of 1943. Our overall organization began to improve in 1944 when there was a rapid increase in artillery pieces, tanks in significant numbers, and the famous Katyushka, a multiple-cannon rocket launcher mounted on a truck. Intelligence services were also making rapid progress, notably in the realm of *razvedka*, or reconnaissance.

I started to wonder how I could escape the infantry and the nightmares of being a foot soldier, those troops fighting without mechanized engines and intended for hand-to-hand combat. Stalin sent infantry to their slaughter with no mercy, not for the dead or wounded and even less for soldiers taken prisoner. We were truly fodder for the cannons. At the end of 1943 I was wounded for the first time, in my right leg, by a mortar shell, and I was evacuated to a hospital behind the front lines where I stayed for three weeks. I was sent back to the front before I was completely healed, and when I returned, I sought a way out of the mud, to join a more specialized unit. Jews made up more than half of our division's force, and I became acquainted with a Jewish lieutenant who was the commander of the reconnaissance and intelligence unit. Since this unit had to cross behind the German front line and bring back information about the enemy's situation back across our own lines, their work was extremely dangerous. It meant getting conclusive evidence of the enemy's strength facing us, where the artillery was located, the number and nature of regiments, and when they had been placed there and then gather whatever other information could be found. Sent out to survey, these units were also trained to capture "tongues" (enemies able to speak) and to sabotage. Bringing back a "tongue," a live German, was the best thing to confirm our intelligence. As you can see, these were risky and, at the same time, complicated actions.

Returning from the hospital, I managed to be recruited into the reconnaissance unit attached to my regiment. As I was still inexperienced, they did not assign me to intelligence missions at first, but instead I was sent on a task that required an experienced horseman. They provided me with a horse to move between units and regiments and keep them in contact with one another during combat. I was also assigned to connect the commander of my regiment and even the division commander with the army commander in the rear, far from the front lines. Some days, the mission required me to ride eighty kilometers. I had hardly been on a horse since I was seven when I had learned on the horse my father owned, and—to tell the truth—my behind was pretty sore at first. In this new section, apart from its commander, there were few Jewish soldiers; they could be counted on one hand. Slowly but surely, I was authorized to take part in intelligence assignments, operations demanding dangerous sorties. I was wounded again during one such operation and transported to the hospital for treatment.

There was an unwritten law among intelligence commandos, that under no circumstance would the wounded be left on the battlefield. We were expected to risk our lives to evacuate wounded comrades back across our lines and were to abandon the dead only if we were absolutely unable to bring them back with us. One day, one of our comrades was wounded two hundred meters from our line, and I volunteered to help him. The only way I could get to him was to crawl on my belly, in the snow in the middle of winter, and under German fire. I slithered toward him, and when I finally reached him I saw that he was mortally wounded in the abdomen by a dum-dum bullet, an expanding munition causing fatal wounds. He insisted that I leave him there because there was no way I could pull him out. But I put him on my back and dragged him along, back across our lines. Sadly, it was only to have him die fifteen minutes later in my arms. Along the path I had taken, a long trail of blood stained the white snow. No engagement ever affected me more. In the eyes of my comrades I was a hero, but inside I felt only terrible and unforgettable fear.

During another reconnaissance mission, I was wounded by a bullet that went through my left leg while I was behind German lines. At night my comrades helped me walk to get back across our line. As soon as I was out of the hospital, I decided that I didn't want to return to this small reconnaissance unit attached to my regiment. Instead, I would join the commando units assigned to reconnaissance and intelligence for the entire division, consisting of 150 men who went out on far more specialized missions. But what strategy should I adopt? How could I make the leap? If I wanted to comply with the official regulations, the preparations would be lengthy ones. But I was young, and with my wound barely healed all I could think of was the idea of accomplishing ever more audacious actions. Like the performer who wants to overcome stage fright, I wanted to conquer my fear and with my hotheaded temperament set my sights on the path of maximum risk.

It so happened that I knew several people in the company. I appeared in front of them and put my request into words, pointing out that I already had some experience with the job. Their commander declared me admitted into their ranks, although normally one wasn't adopted by simple co-optation. By law, I would first have to formulate a request to the section in which I was a combatant and had been wounded, and only after taking this step would I legitimately have the right to transfer. Well, on returning from the hospital, I chose the most illegal and perhaps the most paradoxical route. I deserted my unit and inducted myself into even more dangerous action by never again showing up in my platoon again. Like a submarine I disappeared in one place and reappeared in another. No one really perceived the sleight of hand. In full view of my former commander and former comrades who all believed I was officially detached from my post, and with the blessing of my new hierarchy, I was now fully a member of my new, much more sophisticated company. Reconnaissance commandos were respected by the entire division, and its members had a slight tendency to think of themselves as stars. I must admit that I felt not a little pride, which was piqued whenever I found myself close to my former regiment about to cross to the other side of the lines with my commando comrades. I stayed with this elite company until the end of the war.

We traveled back and forth the entire width of the front and would cross paths with other regiments, companies, and platoons. The work was now much more complex than it had been in my first reconnaissance platoon, where we had at best a pair of binoculars and a compass to orient ourselves and where a mission would last no more than a night. Moving only at night and staying hidden during the day now, we went on sorties lasting several nights. The missions we were assigned demanded the most meticulous preparations. We would stay at our observation posts and carefully study the most trivial facts about the Germans, their slightest gestures, habits, and movements; the number of tanks and artillery pieces at their disposal; anything and everything to pinpoint the strength and disposition of enemy forces. Our investigations were used to draw new maps.

Sometimes, to minimize the risks, we would ask our local artillery unit to organize diversionary fire while we were sneaking in through the enemy lines. Most of the time, we would struggle ahead across woods or marshes. Taking advantage of our artillery's deception, we would thread our way across by a narrow path determined in the course of our long nights' vigil. However, there was no such thing as the perfect route because even if there were no Germans that could be seen, the terrain was terrible and riddled with mines. Our mine-clearing comrades would advance in front of us. Moving only by night, once we had succeeded in penetrating to within a few kilometers of the enemy line, we would move along the edge of the woods and establish ambush posts amid the trees where we remained hidden for the entire day. There in the woods we would complete the information gathering, which we then transmitted by radio when the urgency of the situation called for it. Many of the soldiers who were assigned to building or reestablishing these lines fell on the advanced positions they moved along. In 1943 the front did not move much, and the war had taken on the features of a fixed-in-place war of attrition.

Among the 150 members of our company, only a pair of us were Jews. Most in the company were illiterate. However, they displayed qualities of intelligence, perception, and courage. Many had been taken out of prison by army recruiters; the heads of the army knew that they would find men in prison who had already confronted danger and would not get cold feet. In the commandos, camaraderie was essential and friendships ran deep. Antagonisms and rivalries would have been perilous because we were doomed to face mortal dangers together. We shared whatever we had, in good times and bad. I never sensed any bitter anti-Semitism in the ranks of my unit. But of course, we used to hear in the Red Army—even from those in my regiment—comments that were uncalled for. "The Jews don't go to the front lines and keep themselves hidden in the rear." When I was within hearing range, or a comrade would call me as a witness for what he did or didn't mean, the deprecation was quickly followed with "But you're a good Jew . . . not like the others," as justification and to make sure I didn't retaliate. When fun was made of Jews, it was always in the anodyne form of a joke, thereby avoiding too personal a form. But in truth these insinuations were based on the deeply entrenched anti-Semitism of Russia. We must know of the incredible contributions of our brothers to the battle against Nazism, Hitlerian fascism, as it was called then. A half-million Jews fought in the Red Army, Navy, and Air Force, counting among themselves hundreds of generals and officers of high rank, who distinguished themselves on every front and received the highest awards as heroes of the Soviet army. Out of a total population of three million Jews, it was disproportionate in relation to other populations in the Soviet Union. When we began to move toward Belarus, the Jewish fighters already knew the fate of the Jewish populations. From that point on, we had nothing left to lose and fought with anger and a desire to avenge our martyrs, for the suffering of our families in the hands of their Nazi murderers and the offense against our people.

At reunions of Jewish former combatants in France, in which I long participated as an active member, I have often experienced a patriotism that I understand perfectly well. Jews defend the country in which they live, and in that consists also the greatness of their combat. Neither should we forget the price paid by other Jewish combatants around the world. Yet, at these meetings, I almost never heard any mention of the half-million Jews in the Soviet army. Without the army of the USSR, the most important element in the liberation of Europe, the war might have dragged on forever. Perhaps it is paradoxical, but in every country in the world, we Jews are always the first to burn with the flame of patriotic fervor. During the war of 1914–18, the Jewish patriots of Germany fought those of France. German Jews derived no benefit from it. I must confess patriotism no longer inspires a mystical feeling in me, although I fought on the side of an ideal that proved utopian, or, perhaps because I defended it, it has become difficult for me to reexperience anything like that patriotic fervor.

The Soviet Union lost twenty million people and accepted enormous sacrifices. It is a fact even former Communists dare not remember since the fall of the Berlin Wall. All of Stalin's crimes cannot erase the debt the West owes to Russia. Russians fought in conditions that were unimaginably difficult, not the least of which were the cold and shortages of food. Everything—heavy armor, tanks, transport—was in short supply. And though our clothing may have been warm enough on the Moscow front, going into battle with empty stomachs did not help to conquer the enemy. The war on the Eastern Front went on uninterrupted for a full four years, with fighting that most historians agree was unequaled in ferocity. We need only think of the battles of Leningrad, Stalingrad, and Moscow. In its first year, Stalin's strategy was hamstrung by his own inability to see clearly the disastrous reality. He had completely smashed his own command, annihilated in the purges of the 1930s. Although all of his generals and his agents had seen the attack coming, Stalin chose not to believe them and neglected any preparations. Therefore, when it was unleashed, he changed tactical plans ten times a day as he absorbed the magnitude of the catastrophe washing over the country. My intention is not to criticize the Americans or the British, and especially not the French. But we are obliged to acknowledge that the Allies were late in beginning their offensive in Europe, and for a long time the Russian army stood alone in absorbing the blows of the Germans. Greater men than I have amply established this as fact. Was it political calculation? We should not dismiss the theory. In the end, I maintain that many suffered during the war, but no country suffered as much as Russia, whose territory was devastated all the way to the heart of the Caucasus, as much by Stalin's retreat as by the ferocity of the German offensive. We can never say enough about the infantry divisions that sustained the heaviest losses. As in every war, they were truly the cannon's fodder. After them came the specialized units, the tank, artillery, and antiaircraft crews upon whom the German planes would dive down and strafe with powerful gunfire, targeting as much as possible the special forces supporting the infantry, like engineers, communication, and medical services.

As we know, in retreat, the Russians undertook a scorched-earth policy. This meant that everything, absolutely everything, was put to the torch: fields, cattle, machinery. When we began our counteroffensive, there were no buildings left in which to find shelter. We moved through a desert whose populations had long since been evacuated. From Belarus to the area around Moscow, all territory abandoned by the Russians had suffered the same terrible destruction, giving us a decisive advantage only once the Germans had advanced too far from their bases.

The Soviet army resembled the French army from the point of view of structure and function, except for the presence of political commissars. The General Staff, under the direct orders of Stalin in Moscow, were in charge of the totality of land-based, naval, and air forces. I cannot speak of the navy or air force, which I don't know much about. But the army corps were subdivided into armies merging several divisions, and these in turn were subdivided into battalions made up of four or five specialized regiments. The smallest unit was the platoon. Infantry regiments, the foot soldiers representing the majority of combat regiments and of combat loss, were differentiated by specialization. A given battalion could incorporate an engineering or communications regiment, an artillery regiment, field hospital, NKVD, *khevre-kadishe*,[3] and housekeeping platoons. All platoons had numbers. Every unit had a commandant who might be a party member, although this was not necessarily the case. From the point of view of real power, the political commissar was right behind the commandant. He had something to say on every single issue, and his voice often had more authority than that of the commandant. In theory, he was in charge of the unit's education along political lines, but in practice, he kept his eye on everything, especially the commandant.

Every Russian soldier had a backpack in which he carried his personal items and military gear. From his belt hung bullets and

3. In the original Yiddish text, the author uses the Hebrew/Yiddish word of *khevre-kadishe*, which designates the institution of committed Jews who prepare the body for burial.

grenades, a bayonet and canteen, and, last but not least, his gas mask. In spring and summer, his heavy coat was rolled up and fastened at the shoulder. An essential piece of gear was the small shovel. Weighing at least one kilogram, it enabled us to dig holes for shelter, to protect us from enemy fire. A soldier with a talent for hollowing out these shelters quickly had a chance to stay alive. During the war's first years, when we fought in retreat, we would dig collective trenches. But to ensure more rapid advance when chasing back the Germans, the practice of digging individual holes became standard the moment we began to counterattack. The Soviet army's scorched-earth policy during its retreat had left us with no haven and no roof when our counteroffensive was moving forward. In the summer, to sleep, we fitted out a one-meter-deep shelter, covered it with branches, and that became our home for a few days before we resumed marching. It was called *zemlianka*, from the Russian word for "earth," *zemlia*. In the fall, as the ground began to freeze, digging was no small matter. When winter returned, things were easier since we could dig into the snow and build a kind of igloo. Siberian soldiers, much experienced in matters of low temperatures, taught us their methods. It's hard to conceive how much the snow itself protects against the cold.

Independent of combat, surviving in severe and even extreme temperatures demands an enormous expenditure of energy in and of itself. Malnourished, although fortunately well clothed, we also had to fight. Maneuvers in the snow were laborious and not always in a straight line. Divisions would change their positions depending on tactical considerations. It was common to go on forced marches of forty kilometers a day, in the snow, with empty stomachs because the quartermasters' stores were not forthcoming, while even the horses were stuck in the snow. We were young and strong, sure, but no one gets away from such an ordeal completely unharmed, without experiencing flashback set to go off later as time bombs. In the moment, the necessity of combat made you forget your misery. In my new unit I performed dozens of actions and was wounded four times. But I stayed alive in spite of the dangers facing me. Not everyone was so lucky. Over the four years that I was with the intelligence commandos, hundreds of comrades fell during our operations whom I never saw again. And how many more were wounded?

There were several occasions on which we captured a few Germans—the "tongues"—who were interrogated and confirmed our information. Although I personally never saw torture used on these prisoners, some did sustain beatings.[4] Internal regulations of reconnaissance forces stipulated that all our personal objects, documents, and anything else that could be used to identify us had to be left at the base. Under no circumstances were we to allow ourselves to be identified or our regiment located. No information was allowed to leak. An active commando unit would have between six and ten people. Sometimes in more sophisticated operations, up to fifteen people took part. Most tasks took one night, but if there were woods to provide cover, it might last two or three. We were so used to orienting ourselves at night that we were able to prowl like cats in the dark. Before each operation we had to write a letter that read as follows: "If I am killed during the operation, I ask to be considered among the members of the party." But what would happen if by chance we survived one such dangerous operation? Well, in that case our regiment would simply stamp us as Communists, come what may. Thieves and hoodlums, who were not in short supply among us, were no exception to the rule, and with party card in their pockets, they too became respectable Communists.

It must not be forgotten that the SMERSH, the military branch of NKVD units, was responsible for internal security and had agents planted in every single unit.[5] They had a file relating to every soldier and every officer. They were the ones who took care of deserters, returning them to their units for a public execution after undergoing

4. Moishe Rozenbaumas was always firm and coherent about this fact, only conceding that the beatings for militaries at war in such a context were severe.

5. Joseph Stalin coined the name СМЕРШ (SMERSH) as a portmanteau of the phrase Смерть шпионам (*Smert shpionam*, "Death to Spies").

an expedited court-martial. When someone committed a serious offense, or so considered by their book, he was turned over to a *strafnaya rota*, a punishment regiment, which would be placed on the front line during an attack. In these conditions, the chance of staying alive was minimal, and though some did survive, they were usually wounded, and thus paid for their offense with their blood.

According to established rules, I was too young to belong to the party. It usually required an additional two or three years following membership in the young Communist organizations, the *komsomols*. First, one had to submit an application and undergo a probationary period. Then one submitted a new application, for full membership this time. However, my regiment waived the rules. Things happened that way. It's a delusion to think that everyone was a Communist in the Soviet Union—far from it. Out of a total of nearly two hundred million people, approximately seven million were party members. In civilian life, a party member had a lot of privileges. On the other hand, belonging to the party brought a soldier no advantage—quite the contrary. It forced on him a duty to always be first, the first to accept an operation at the front of an infantry attack, the first to yell "hurrah" while running ahead of the others on the battlefield, the first one to die with party honors. Our regiment, which was 80 percent Communist, had seen its numbers turn over more than ten times. By war's end, a minuscule group of veterans remained alive. From the vicinity of Moscow to Germany, the road was long and covered not with flowers but with the blood that flowed like rivers, the agony of the hundreds of soldiers fallen in the battles. More than fifty years later, my dreams are haunted by these images. The remembrance of my fallen comrades still appears to me.

The 16th Lithuanian Division was an infantry corps composed of Lithuanians, Russians, and numerous Jews. Those who survived know well how excruciating was the road back for us Lithuanian Jews. The liberation of Lithuania was an ordeal. When we arrived, it was to find our houses emptied of our families, who had vanished, and occupied by Lithuanians. When I reached Telz, my first instinct was to run to my house. I pounced on it like a madman. I found not one living soul, not my mother and not my brothers. At that time, my father was not even in my mind. I thought only of my mother and my three brothers. Had I been a civilian, I would not even have been able to set foot inside the house. I was arriving as a liberator after four years of war, and the people who occupied my home looked on me as nothing but an invader, though they were trembling. They knew nothing and had seen nothing. They had been allocated the apartment, whose furniture had been pillaged before they moved in. That same day, I learned where our families had been massacred. There is no way to describe my rage and my sorrow. My heart cried out for vengeance. And vengeance was taken, on the Germans and later on their Lithuanian henchmen, who had murdered my people and my family, exterminated the greater part of the Jews of Telz and of all Lithuania. The Jews who survived were mostly those who fled with the Russian army or had joined the 16th Division.

Writing about oneself is obviously more difficult than writing about others, and I'm not inclined to dwell on my own case. I know that up until March 1945, when I was wounded for the last time, I had fought with loyalty, faithfulness, and commitment. My first combat had been in front of Moscow, defending the cities of Orel and Tula. Then we liberated Belarus and Lithuania, and after that we broke through the German lines near Tilsit and Königsberg. I received my fourth and last wound on the Nieman, in eastern Prussia, not far from Memel, where I had been born. For me, the war was now over. I was sent to a field hospital, not far from Telz, where I grew up. Once again, I had been wounded in the leg, but I quickly did my best to walk on crutches.

The Russian regional commandant was looking for trustworthy translators. Part of the effort to pursue and bring to justice war criminals required fluent Lithuanian as much as it did Russian. The NKVD found me at the hospital and wanted to co-opt me into the job. We were to interrogate suspects, collaborators, members of the Nazi Fifth Column, Lithuanian fascists belonging to the Ypatingasis būrys

(Special Squad),[6] the executioners of the Jewish population. Although the war was not over, I was not being sent back to the front. It was not in their power to force me to participate in this kind of work. They asked me if I would volunteer to help. The decision was easy. My deepest wound was not in the leg. We went into villages and rural areas, where we flushed out the war criminals in hiding. My job was to interrogate them, and after that they were judged before a somewhat expedited military tribunal and in most cases condemned to death. They were shot sometime the same day. Among the criminals arrested in Telz was the murderer of my younger brother Leybe, who actually may have been his playmate. When the Jewish men and boys had been gathered at Rainiai,[7] the place planned for their massacre, he led him and some other boys to believe that he would help them escape. They had not gone fifty meters when this same boy mowed them down with a machine gun. Only one boy of this group survived, wounded, and managed to save himself, and his testimony was confirmed to me by the crime's mastermind. He had participated in the town's mass killings and used as his mistress a beautiful Jewish girl of fifteen or sixteen whom he ended up murdering, shooting her in the head. He was judged and condemned to death. His was the only execution I attended. My mother had been murdered at Geruliai along with the women and the youngest children. Seven thousand women and children from the area were murdered in a trench 120 meters long. The killing went on for weeks, and the testimony of local peasants recalled the cries, the tears, the open pits, and the nearby stream running with blood. In five pits at Rainiai,

6. See Michael MacQueen, "Lithuanian Collaboration in the 'Final Solution': Motivations and Case Studies," in *Lithuania and the Jews: The Holocaust Chapter*, symposium presentations, United States Holocaust Memorial Museum, 2005, https://web.archive.org/web/20060515225310/http://www.ushmm.org/research /center/publications/occasional/2005-07-03/paper.pdf.

7. Concerning the massacre places of the Telzer Jewish men, women, and children, please see the editor's website, http://batkamaat.org/?page_id=2212.

four thousand men and youth were murdered. One group of men was led to Rainiai on their knees. This was told to me on my arrival in Telz by a group of Lithuanians, a fact not subsequently recorded in the Memorial Book of Telz. And a short distance away, the last five hundred girls, who had been locked up in an improvised ghetto near the lake, were exterminated on Christmas night, 1941.[8]

Our division had liberated Lithuania, but the offensive had continued without pause. Until the end of the war, the advance was very rapid and did not leave enough time even to gather in memory of them at the places where we knew our families had been murdered. Having been wounded at the end of the war was my special privilege, allowing me to work as a translator for the NKVD in the hunt for criminals when the war was still going on. From what I could judge, the NKVD did a good job in hunting down the criminals and chief collaborators, yet the trials were cursory and the right to a defense was not ensured. The Russians had also seen entire families wiped out, torched and murdered, and the rage toward the Germans and their henchmen was indescribable. Russian losses had no equal. But even if they practiced only a cursory form of justice, the Russians never killed the German prisoners in cold blood. It was strictly forbidden by the military command, even more so the killing of women and children. Nevertheless, cases of women being raped under threat were unfortunately not rare. I was an eyewitness to one myself. These were not "punitive rapes," like those in Yugoslavia's recent war,[9] but came from a lack of discipline linked to the personal frustration of the soldiers.

My work with the NKVD lasted until the end of the war, and it was under these circumstances that I met people from Telz who had survived, hidden by peasants in the city's outskirts. Because it was

8. See http://batkamaat.org/?page_id=3198.

9. The time period was 1990–92. This statement about the motivations of the rapes was a controversial discussion between the author and his daughter, the editor of the present version. The phrasing reflects strictly Moishe Rozenbaumas's own terms.

almost impossible for a man to find a hiding place, most survivors were women. I helped them mostly by finding food for them, the rarest of commodities until the end of the war. I saw some of these survivors again on subsequent visits to Israel, and we shared great joy in seeing each other again. One of the women, ninety-six years old as I write this, lives in a retirement home and shows me great affection, always calling me by my pet name, Meyshl.

2. Mozes Rozenbaum, Moishe's paternal grandfather.

3. Clara Steinbock.

4. Clara Steinbock, Moishe's paternal grandmother, sitting near her son, Itzik Rozenbaum.

5. Aaron Meyerowitz, Moishe's maternal grandfather.

6. Tsivia Meyerowitz, née Ackerman, Moishe's maternal grandmother.

7. Mere-Khaye Meyerowitz, Moishe's mother.

8. Moishe (born 1922), sitting near his father and mother, and Leybe (born 1924) on his father's knees, around 1929, with three cousins from Riteve.

9. Yosef (born 1919), Moishe's older brother, sitting near a friend on May 17, 1935.

10. Leybe and Elie (born 1931), Moishe's younger brothers.

11. Rosa Portnoi, Debiosi, 1941.

12. Rosa, with her friend Sonia, in Debiosi (the Urals), end of 1941.

13. Rosa and Moishe after the war, around the time of their wedding.

14. Rosa and Moishe with Sacha, around 1949.

15. Rosa and Moishe with Sacha, around 1950.

16. Moishe with Sacha, May 1953.

17. Family picture in front of the Gediminas Tower, 1954.

18. Rosa with Sacha and Isabelle, spring 1954.

19. Sacha and Isabelle.

20. May 1 in the Laisvé factory (*Moishe first from right, Rosa third*).

21. Moishe (*middle*) with workers in the Voum Kombinat workshop shortly after he resigned from the vocational school.

22. Summer gathering (*Moishe, standing second on the right, Rosa sitting on the left with Sacha standing*), August 11, 1952.

23. Photo taken in Pompeii when Moishe was reunited with his father, Yitzkhak, early April 1957.

24. Françoise, Moishe's little sister, at age nine when he met her in France.

Return to Life—L'chaim

When the war was over I returned to my unit, where we proceeded to celebrate our victory. Each of us received a letter signed by Stalin himself, in recognition of our participation in the war of 1939–45. The only thing I would hold on to from the war, other than my decorations, was the habit of consuming a lot of alcohol, regardless of what it was called, its strength, or its quality. Vodka was by far my favorite, but no one was very particular in those days, and, in an era of shortages, cologne served the purpose very well. I needed the burning sensation it gave me, the forgetting of sorrows, of difficult days, of privations endured and battlefield horrors.

You might wonder how a young man who had never been a serious drinker—and Jews were not great consumers of alcohol—had devoted himself to this twisted passion that began with army conscription and continued right up until turning into a seasoned alcoholic. To understand, we have to turn back to an earlier chapter. When we were in front of Moscow in 1942, the temperature never climbed above minus thirty degrees Celsius, which made our bones literally feel like they were cracking. This winter was exceptional even for Russia. The gusts of wind were so cold that they glued the frost to your face. Spit from your mouth arrived on the ground frozen. Under such conditions, every soldier had a right to one hundred grams per day of vodka. Officers were allotted two hundred grams per day, as were we, in our reconnaissance units, because our work was considered both risky and grueling. You had to be ready to lay down your life with each and every mission. However, while out on an operation even one drop was strictly forbidden. But when we left on missions lasting four or five days—including the time of preparation, we still accumulated our off-duty rations—our vodka was waiting for us when we got back. We drank it all upon returning, along with the rations of dead or wounded comrades, who made up the majority. We were constantly on the move, and the missions followed one upon another. It was rare to stay on base for more than three or four days, but in their way those days were equally lethal, because no one prevented us from calming our anxiety and fear by absorbing our accumulated rations. We drank, we sang, we partied, forgetting for a few days what we were living through. A young man inured to his drink can tolerate incredible amounts of alcohol, up to one liter at a sitting. In the long run, it becomes a penetrating need, and the cold no longer had anything to do with it. We procured the elixir even in summer when it was no longer distributed. Except for the boys who were lucky enough to be unable to tolerate alcohol, every soldier among us consumed enormous quantities of alcohol.

As I wrote, our division liberated Lithuania but didn't have any time to stop in our towns while on the offensive. Once the war ended our division returned to Vilna, now the capital of the Lithuanian Soviet Socialist Republic. A big parade was organized in our honor, and we changed into our ceremonial uniforms, which hadn't been worn during the entire four years of fighting. With our decorations and polished boots shining like mirrors, we cut a fine figure as we marched in step to the sound of a military orchestra. With flowers and applause, the people greeted us as liberators, crying "Bravo!" But if one bothered to analyze this reaction, the reality was different. A large percentage of the population had collaborated with the Germans and had no love for the uniform of Soviet soldiers.

Our unit was stationed on Vilnius's outskirts, others were billeted in surrounding areas, and several large units were stationed in other cities, such as Kaunas, the former capital, as well as Šiauliai and Klaipeda. Our unit was exempted from drills, and we began to feel like we were on vacation. The former vanguard that we had been, exposed to so much danger, was relishing the taste of our newly granted freedom of movement. In the immediate aftermath of the war, the one great problem was the procurement of vodka. The war was over, it was the middle of summer, and the commandant was no longer distributing it. We were therefore reduced to looking for expedients to obtain our medicine. This was, of course, not entirely in accord with the law. First we sold military uniforms, even our own, then cigarettes. Next we began trafficking in railroad tickets. Getting from one city to another had become an obstacle course, and one had to wait in a line for hours to buy tickets. But the decorations on our chest allowed us to go to the front of the line, and then we sold the tickets for a healthy profit margin. With the ill-gotten money, we would let loose, *men hot gemakht a lebn*; we lived it up and partied hard. Time passed quickly, and at that moment we had no other worries and no military assignments either.

Our drills had still not restarted, and we were as free as fish in water. One fine day, I was walking through downtown, on Pylimo Street, when I noticed two women talking. I looked carefully at the one with her back turned to me, who was wearing a striped burgundy raincoat that I had already seen somewhere. My eyes, those of the tailor and the army scout, could not be mistaken. I was so used to retaining details and colors that I was wrong only one time in a hundred. And so I screwed up all my courage and walked up to the little red coat and gave it a friendly pat on the shoulder. A young lady turned around, and then I could see that I was not wrong. I recognized Reyzele from Telz. My destiny was waiting for me on this street corner. Our surprise at meeting again after such a long four-year war was tremendous, and our joy was no less.

I learned how she had fled from Telz with her parents and family, at first on virtually the same route as mine, and how they became refugees deep inside Russia, in the Urals. In 1943 I had met two of her sisters who were drafted in the army and been transferred into our division. From them I received news of their family, particularly of Reyzele, as well as their address. It is how I sent a few words on the back of a photograph that showed me on horseback, taken on the battlefield. The picture was tiny, about five by ten centimeters, but I managed to inscribe on this tiny surface what resembled a little poem in Yiddish. The dedication on the back stated forthrightly: "I can offer you nothing nicer and nothing better / I'm sending my photo for you to remember / And if ever you long for some memory of mine / Be reminded that Meyshke is my name."

> 13-8-43
> *keyn sheyners un keyn besers ken ikh dir nit shenken*
> *ikh shenk dir mayn bild du zolst mir gedenkn*
> *un az du vest zikh veln on mir dermonen*
> *zolstu visn az Meyshke is may nomen.*

Notice that in spite of my modest education, I demonstrated a certain inclination toward "poetic" expression. I'm joking, of course. To be truthful, I hadn't given any thought to the future at the time I sent it. Once again, you have to believe that whatever destiny has in store for you, it will ultimately happen. And this is true even if you remained warm in a blanket and didn't budge. My wife saved the picture, kept it always with her, and still has it sixty years later.

Reyzele invited me into the family home that was, *bli eyn hore,* may God protect them from evil, filled with children, seven girls and a boy.[1] I was very kindly received. Supply problems were acute, and even basic necessities were lacking. Bread, meat, sugar, and dairy products along with many others items were rationed. The same thing went for coal and firewood. The few stores in existence were half empty. For any purchase of an essential product, one had to present a ration card. I really couldn't begin to understand how Rosa, who was the eldest child, was able to manage, but she had probably put everything the family owned on their little table. There was a carafe of more than a liter of vodka—could it be that no one else was drinking?—cucumbers, and a lot of sour cream. I may have been literally pickled in alcohol, but in four years I had not as much as seen

---

1. Rosa, born in 1921; Sara/Sonke, b. 1924; Mina, b. 1926; Nekhemye, b. 1928; Galia, b. 1932; Perke, b. 1936; Louba, b. 1940; and Rokhl, b. 1941.

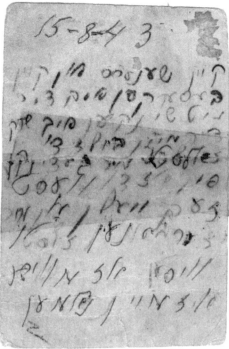

25. Moishe dispatched in the 16th Division; photo sent to Rosa on August 15, 1943, with a poem on the back.

26. Autographed poem sent to Rosa, August 15, 1943.

a cucumber, let alone a pot of sour cream. Had I been observant, at that moment I would have said the *shekheyonu*, the blessing said each year on the early harvest, or spontaneously at the happy occasion of any first time, or at a holiday festive period inauguration. I was the only one who ate while the others were simply watching. The spread seemed insufficient for such a large family. They couldn't allow themselves to take part in such a meal, but they had wanted to receive me in a dignified style. For me it was a feast. At another time or in another place, it might have spoiled my appetite to eat alone in front of others, but it was not the case on that day. Not because I was badly raised or selfish—on the contrary. I always enjoyed sharing whatever I had with others. But I understood their feeling of unease, perhaps their embarrassment. And so, talking all the while, I finished the carafe of vodka along with the cucumbers and cream. The meal over, I thanked my hosts for their warm welcome. I'm sure they were expecting me to collapse as soon I stood up. Not only didn't I fall, but I stood practically erect while continuing the conversation pretty normally. I was especially careful to conduct myself as someone who was well brought up. I was used to drinking a lot, but I would have paid any price to not have them think they were dealing with a drunk.

As I learned later, I had fooled no one, and the family concluded they should be wary of me. During this first visit, I had been won over by the kindness and great heart of Reyzele's mother, a modest and simple authentic *yiddishe mame* who didn't talk much or ask any questions.

And so, after dinner, I politely took my leave and got back to my unit on the other side of town. I met Reyzele several times after that, while I was still a soldier, and continued visiting her family, sometimes in the company of my best friends. My two comrades belonged to the same unit, one a lieutenant and the other a sergeant, and besides their other decorations, they wore the highest civilian and military honor, the gold Hero of the Soviet Union star, which conferred incalculable privileges from which they profited amply. Once we stayed drunk for three days and three nights at Reyzele's house. She had unearthed for us a small room on the first floor of a neighboring apartment. We were so drunk we fell asleep on the floor. To justify ourselves, we pretended we were celebrating the end of the war, an excuse as good as any other. But I was going to have to think about sobering up to face the impending day of a return to civilian life and becoming a *mentsh*. I don't know who had protected me during the war, but now I would have to make sure I was protected from myself and start a family.

Reyzele's mother was a modest woman; she was poor and unacquainted with hypocrisy, a remarkable person with a heart of gold and touching generosity and kindness. She would give up her last morsel of bread without expecting any thanks. With eight children and a sick husband in the house, she was the one who ran around to feed her family and had a kind word for everyone. I never heard her complain about her material condition or about her health. I loved her for real, in earnest. As a way of cutting up among family, I used to say that it was because of her mother that I married my wife.

My mother-in-law played a significant role in a memorable episode of my life. Out of decency, when I wrote the initial Yiddish draft of this text, I was reticent to recount the incident that occurred while I was still in the army. I was at a wedding and the celebration was in full swing, the wedding party having drunk an unreasonable amount. It was five in the morning, and the doors were wide open, as was the custom, when four Lithuanian policemen burst in and began disrupting the party. The hosts tried coaxing them with food and drink, but quickly, anti-Semitic insults were being hurled, and the guests became frightened. I was the only man in military uniform, covered with decorations and armed with my pistol, but that did not stop them from provoking me. First I asked them to leave, but their answer was to insult me and beat me up. I had also drunk more than a few glasses and not thimble-size ones. I took out my revolver and began defending myself, and in spite of my drunkenness I didn't fire but used the butt end only. Without looking, I struck where I could, but there were too many of them. The guests were petrified. I was successful in keeping my cool and did not open fire. I fought until I received a head wound and started to bleed. But their words hurt more. At the sight of blood they left, but not before they had relieved me of my firearm. I was taken care of as if I was the Messiah, and only then could the party go on. I felt a sort of euphoria from having been able to defend the group and left the hall at six in the morning walking in the direction of my predestined Reyzele. In spite of the first aid I had received, I was still losing blood, and not ten meters from the house, I collapsed on the sidewalk. I don't know how long I lay unconscious. Reyzele's mother, by chance, was going out and found me. At first sight, she thought I was dead. She managed to have me brought home and succeeded in stopping the bleeding. Later on, I was able to return to the barracks with a bloodied bandage around my head.

After examining the wound, my friends, and especially my lieutenant (the Hero of the Soviet Army), questioned me, demanding to know what had been done with my pistol. After thinking it over, they decided to avenge the honor of the regiment and recover the weapon. They organized what amounted to a real military action, a raid on the commissariat of police. The only thing we didn't have was an artillery piece, but that is a weapon reconnaissance units did not possess. Here we are taking off in the middle of the day, twenty strapping guys aboard a truck and armed for battle. The encirclement of the building was accomplished in the blink of an eye. We demanded that all police personnel be lined up, and the four guilty parties, who were as worked over as I was, were briskly identified. To put it bluntly, they got what was coming to them, followed by their apologies. The four malefactors were fired from the police force, and my revolver was returned. Immediately after the war, the army took precedence over the police, as this event made clear. I was confronted with anti-Semitism three other times, in the presence of Reyzele before our wedding and two times after that.

An order came down from the army that stipulated that a soldier who had been wounded more than three times had the right to ask to be demobilized. I didn't wait a day longer and was demobilized the very day I applied. My only wealth was my backpack, although I also had taken one German trophy, a big NSU motorcycle equipped with a sidecar and a beautiful new spare motor. The motor was so powerful that ten or more of us would climb aboard, but I had to store my cumbersome bike where my unit was posted because I had no housing as of yet. I did manage to make good use of it later on. Other than official vehicles, Vilnius had no cars or motorbikes after the war.

It did not take long for Reyzele and me to decide to get married. And no sooner had we decided than we faced a pitfall. Rosa was very observant, while I was one of those atheistic Communists indoctrinated with Marxism-Leninism and—to state the plain truth—with Stalinism as well. Nothing in life is straightforward. Reyzele wanted a religious ceremony, one that adhered to the rituals of Jewish law, with the rabbi and the *khupe*, the wedding canopy. No more and no less. From this she would never back down. For a Communist this was . . . pure heresy, but she remained firm, proud and inflexible, more inflexible than the Red Army and Communist Party put together. My destiny was waiting for me, so my only option was surrender. On November 7, 1945, the anniversary of the Russian Revolution and a public holiday, we were married in Vilnius's very last synagogue, where Reyzele worked as the rabbi's secretary, Rabbi Ausband[2]—from Telz—who gave us *khupe vekdushe*, pronounced the nuptial blessing. Rosa's aunt, Feyge-Heyne, and her uncle lived on the Neris, also called the Vilya, the river that went through the town. There they organized a small and charming party for us and entertained about twenty people. We danced to the sounds of an accordion, until the party finally ended, late at night.

Half of Vilnius, especially the streets of the former ghetto, had been destroyed by the Germans. With the party's help, I had obtained a small two-room apartment located near the town center, no easy feat. I wasn't looking for work yet and spent my time with friends who were still in the army. We went out dancing a lot. In short, our minds were set on having fun. Everyone needed to forget. But you can't survive on love, fresh air, and vodka alone. It was becoming urgent to start thinking about working. It was late 1945, and all my friends from the army had obtained important jobs. I won't even mention those who were party members. The first ones named to important jobs were Lithuanians, followed by the Russians, and, last, with the exception of those who had been party members before the Russians arrived, came the Jews. I contacted the central committee of the Lithuanian Communist Party, which had an employment service, and without further delay I was made vice director of a vocational

2. Rabbi Aizik Ausband, the last remaining rabbi from the original group of rabbis that reestablished the Telzer Yeshiva in Cleveland, died recently. He was ninety-six. Student of the Telzer Yeshiva in 1932, he married one of the daughters of the rabbinical family Bloch, Chaya Bloch. See also the editor's website, http://batkamaat.org/?attachment_id=1538. Rabbi Aizik Ausband will have a part later in this narrative. See also note 1 in the chapter "My Father, My Wife, and My Star."

school. Considering my military record and my decorations, I could have gotten an even higher-level position, but my education was limited, and so I accepted this work, aware of my limitations and everything that I would have to learn. The job was slightly out of town, on the banks of the little Vileyka, a tributary of the Neris. As part of my assignment, they provided me a four-room apartment near work. At that time, most families often shared a common kitchen, so this vast flat for only two persons represented a luxury.

As for our move, it was practically over before it started . . . Other than two chairs, a bed, and a small table, we owned no furniture and no wardrobe. We were now living on the outskirts of Vilnius in a three-story building with a courtyard backing onto the river. We occupied a raised ground-floor apartment reached by climbing six steps. Reyzele planted flowers in the small garden out front.[3] When the ice melted in springtime, the river became dangerous, swelling and tripling its flow. But in the summer, the children swam in the river and went "boating" in washtubs. In winter you could ski or sled down the slopes of the opposite bank.

---

3. And where Moishe has planted a tree. The building and what was left (in 2000–2001) of this industrial neighborhood can be seen in the film of Isabelle Rozenbaumas and Michel Grosman, *Nemt: A Language without a People for a People without a Language*, at about seven to eight minutes from the beginning: http://batkamaat.org/?page_id=43.

Swimming in Troubled Waters; or, The Rules of Peace

My work was just steps away from the house. As assistant director, I was provided with my own office, a secretary, and a phone, which was not very common just after the war. The school was a vocational college that provided instruction for all sorts of trades, such as plumbing, mechanics, welding, electricity, locksmithing, tailoring and garment cutting, radio repair, iron working, the building trades, and others. The school's director had two assistant directors, one responsible for theoretical and technical studies, and me, in charge of provisioning and supplying the school with whatever was necessary for the classes and the boarding school to function, such as heating and food, in addition to clothing and uniforms for the personnel and the three hundred students and teachers.

I saw to the coal orders that kept the central heating going and watched over all work and nearly everything else going on inside and outside the building. It was a big responsibility, made even bigger after the war, because in every domain supplies were chaotic and insufficient and all distribution relied on a system of ration cards. Nevertheless, I was quick to understand that one hand must ignore what the other one does. If I didn't, what I would be able to procure would be strictly zilch. In this return to a barter economy, circulating money had become a thing of the past, and the limits of what was legal or illegal were extremely tenuous. There was no other realistic way of obtaining supplies.

There were only boys in this institution. The most urgent need was, as the rules prescribed, to clothe them. So I had uniforms made for students and staff, as well as for myself. These uniforms were aqua blue with gold buttons and matching caps. They looked almost identical to the uniforms of the police or those of military aviators; the only thing missing were epaulettes. Myself, I was only exchanging one uniform for another.

At around the same time, I also went to take possession of my motorcycle, with its enormous thousand-cubic-centimeter engine. My service revolver was still with me. I had not handed it in because it had never been listed as a part of the unit's inventory. I had taken it off of a German officer in 1943 and had never been separated from it since, carrying it without a permit, strapped to the back on my right side. All the policemen manning the intersections would look at me with respect when I went through town, convinced that I occupied an elevated position in the police leadership, never failing to salute me as one of their own. They acted the same way when I was on foot. It didn't hurt that my chest was full of medals, pinned to the brand-new uniform I was wearing.

Given the situation brought about by the war, my work was nothing less than a godsend. At a time when everything was scarce, the students were sheltered from need and had whatever was necessary. The government provided quantities of merchandise, but some were in excess and others insufficient. Barter was an objective necessity. The state provided the school with bread, butter, flour, sugar, some canned vegetables, and even cake and chocolate. The school also owned an agricultural plant and farm about ten kilometers from the city. I was completely responsible for it and had designated a director who was assisted by a very small staff to take care of it. The farm was not big and consisted of a few outbuildings and two hectares of land. It supplied our potatoes and vegetables throughout the year. The staff did the planting and looked after the crops, while the students came in rotations to do the harvesting.

The essential thing was procuring the coal to run the heating system and the kitchen. The canteen was organized as a restaurant, running at full capacity three times a day, and did not lack for enlightened amateurs whose uninterested visits were ostensibly to see how we were doing. The dining hall attracted people like honey attracts flies. As the school lacked a transportation mode, I procured a twenty-ton Mercedes truck using my army acquaintances as inter-mediaries in the deal. With the truck, I could bring in the eighty wagons of coal we were allocated. In the winter, it was more precious than bread. Since the work was not mechanized, every day I had to assign a group of pupils to load and unload the truck by shovel.

Without standing on ceremony, the director had given me a list of party cadres, generals, and party personalities to whose homes I was to deliver coal. Afterward, members of the Department of Education, on whom we were dependent, came to present their own entreaties. Then, by word of mouth, other ministers of other departments, not to mention party members who had not made it onto our lists, all spoke to our director. It was never possible to refuse. I invited the solicitors to sit down and asked them what they required. It was commonplace for them to ask for a ton of coal, and I would open my dumbfounded eyes and tell them that unfortunately I was not able to supply such quantities. I would then suggest half that amount. We often didn't know for sure who we were dealing with, and to utter the word "no" in front of these people was not an option. In such delicate, opaque situations, as we were even clueless as to what was the quid for our pro in the barter, speaking about money would have been not only bad taste but off-topic—because we had no right to sell, had no cash, and didn't even keep any books. The beneficiaries of these free deliveries were aware that these practices were in vio-lation of the law and never thanked us. The director would merely send them to see me, asking me to do my best by them. On me he dumped the task of responding or not to the requests and squabbling over the quantity of coal each was to receive. Thus diverted as a favor to private individuals, the coal was not brought in or taken out of the school, but allocated and delivered directly from the freight station. The school required only sixty wagons of coal, so part of the surplus was used as a means of barter. For example, opposite the school was a lemonade factory that had surplus sugar but was short of coal to heat their pots. We didn't really need the sugar, but we traded our coal for their sugar, because we could use it to get more bread or something else we lacked. My students were drinking free lemonade year-round.

We lived three hundred meters from the school, and because it was still very hard to get a telephone line hooked up, I hung a wire between the school and our apartment. For the next three years until I left the school, every time the phone rang in my office it rang in my home at the same time. That ended precisely on the day when my little boy took the apparatus apart with a screwdriver.[1]

The entire system was built on and supported by illegal, dishonest, and immoral operations known to all those with any stake in the system but that everyone pretended to ignore. As they say in Russia, "No wind, no news, no idea." No one uttered a word. My position made it impossible for me not to participate, and moreover I still had an army state of mind with a certain taste for risk and cunning. I took things way too far, caught up in the whirlwind. I never looked back on whatever occurred and acted like the others, even if these dealings left an unpleasant aftertaste. The situation in Lithuania was not comparable to the one in the other former Soviet republics. The state had just barely been established, and notwithstanding the fear that everyone inspired in his neighbor, immense anarchy ruled. Everyone strove for a place at the table. From top to bottom, the totality of administrative posts was run by former military men who acted as though the war wasn't over. Furthermore, the officers all knew each other and continued to trade favors and services as before. When the state started to consolidate itself, these practices became more covert and more hypocritical, no longer a question of barter but now one of blatant theft, where only those who were in the upper castes went unpunished.

Our house was always full of people, some to sleep, some to eat, and some to do both. The family would come over to eat and drink,

---

1. This little boy, Alexandre (Sacha), was born in June 1946. It says all about the engineering brain he inherited from the Apple Thief.

glasses clinking, l'chaim (to life!) resonating. Most of the time our guests were Russian, so Russian had the upper hand in the incessant toasting, and we heard a lot of *za vashe zdarovie*, "to your health." Rosa preferred that we drink at home and not outside because she would have some control over the situation and the amounts ingested. Most of the guests were army buddies who had not yet been demobilized and remained voluntarily under the colors. Besides our direct family circle, distant relatives were now reaching out to us. Our connections were multiplying. Echoes from our table reached to the provinces, and people from our native region coming to Vilnius to take care of business would arrive with their suitcases, to spend the night at our house and, needless to say, to eat and drink. My wife had a lot to do, but she was young and spirited and never grumbled. Her numerous sisters sometimes came to help out, but still, under the circumstances, we had to hire a live-in maid. It was not usually easy to get a girl from the countryside and to have her passport stamped with authorization to live in the city because the state did not want peasants leaving the land and invading the city, least of all the capital. And when the girls wanted to leave us and find work in the factories, I had to start the process all over again.

Much has been written about the Soviet Union. All kinds of specialists, political scientists, sociologists, thinkers, and ordinary citizens have all expressed an opinion. Everyone tells the story in his own way and with his own interpretation of events. I myself can only speak of my own experience. I am not pretending here to be giving a historical analysis, nor will I describe the entire reality of the era. Nobody holds the truth in his hand. What I can say is that in 1945, I was still a dedicated Communist and had no doubt as to the necessity of building a society with more justice for the majority of the population. At that time I knew nothing of the trials of the 1930s, and during the first years after the war I was shaped and educated from *A* to *Z* by the party. I believed in a better future for the working classes among whom I had grown up. As I explained, I was twenty-two when I joined the party during the war, when doing so conferred no privilege but imposed on me only a patriotic duty. The army had instilled in us discipline, obedience, responsibility, and a desire to always set an example. Most soldiers were not party members. But after the war, the situation changed radically. In the "liberated" territories, like Lithuania, there was a power vacuum. In the cities and towns where governmental and civil infrastructure did not exist, the Communist organizations appointed managers and party members to come to grips with settling civilian life, because the civil service remnants still in place had massively and zealously collaborated with the Nazis. The Germans had ruled for four years.

Everything needed rebuilding. In the absence of trained cadres, priority was given to appointing demobilized soldiers of the Lithuanian division. Still young, and having gone through four years of war, it would be untrue to say that these men were trained for administrative work. Two or three years would be necessary in order for this generation of new officials to learn something of organizational matters.

Let me explain how the party was organized. Appointed by Moscow, the Central Committee of the Lithuanian Communist Party adopted the well-tried methods of the Soviet Union. All civilian entities took their orders from the Central Committee. Directives came down the rungs of the party organization, passing through party committees in the city, neighborhood districts, and so on, down to the smallest cell at the base. The initial elections took place in these cells. If they elected a secretary who was a Lithuanian, his deputy had to be a Russian. The same thing applied to elections higher up the scale. Nothing was left to chance. On the contrary, everything unfolded according to an agenda minutely worked out in advance. Candidates were always named beforehand by the next-highest authority, and no one would have even known how to put forth whatever he had in mind or crossed his imagination that was not already the party line. There was no question of showing the remotest flexibility, budging an inch one way or another, and woe to anyone who transgressed this unwritten law. Being a party member straight from military life, where we had been blinded by this deceptively democratic comedy, I was still naïve and did not see the perverse effects of this charade. I thought everything was working wonderfully.

The unions and professional organizations, in which at the least the secretary or the president was a member of the party, served as transmission conduits. In a factory or a bureaucracy, elections were held once a year for the union committee followed by its president. To this end one person, a party member, it goes without saying, was first named to lead the union electoral assembly. A few exceptional "spontaneous" candidates were allowed to run in the elections, but we just allegedly voted for the first name proposed by the electoral assembly. The workers, sick of meetings, did not venture to show up. The few innocents who stood up to speak got nowhere. Once his contingent of handpicked candidates was ready, the president of the electoral process would expertly shut off the list of committee candidates. These maneuvers were so well prepared and so well naturally executed that the ordinary worker had no time to think or react. You could be inside the system or outside of it, but you could not oppose it.

In the factories, *kombinats*,[2] *kolkhozes*, and other organizations, directors and their deputies were chosen by the party through the ministry to which they belonged. Most were party members, while others were the experts needed for the enterprise but who, to hold on to their jobs, took no time in joining it. In addition to this standard mix, nationalities and the question of "Russification" of the Soviet republics also imposed itself. In the immediate aftermath of the war, the marching orders were "national cadres first," which, in Lithuania, might have meant a citizen who was born in Lithuania, which would have included Russians, Poles, and Jews. However, this pronouncement remained only loosely interpreted, because the prime positions were shared between Russians and Lithuanians, followed by Jews and Poles. In Lithuania the party secretary was a Lithuanian

---

2. *Kombinat*: economic entity of industrial or service nature consisting of several specialized, technologically related enterprises.

and his deputy a Russian. Don't forget that the propaganda and bogus news apparatus was claiming, in unflappable doublespeak, that the Lithuanians were at the helm of the society. The personality cult around Stalin was used to plant these "truths" in the hearts of the multitude. Nothing began or ended without the words of Stalin, homages to his greatness, and praises of his good deeds, past, present, and future. No lone peccadillo could be dealt with or resolved without exalting Stalin's merits. He was as omnipresent as an ancient god, an idol, or an icon.

Even though the official language was Lithuanian, all public texts were written in Russian, owing to the many Russians "parachuted" into the country who could neither speak Lithuanian nor much less write it. They were there to Russify Lithuania, the identical plan being applied in every one of the Soviet republics. It speaks a lot to the amount of resentment that the Russians left in their wake. It was this same outrageous policy that, without realizing, I had paid for with my own suffering in Uzbekistan, where we were considered Russian.

There was iron discipline within the party. You could join it, but if you wanted to leave, the road out went through Siberia. Or if a little mistake got you thrown out, then *okh un vey*, woe to you, you were marked for life. Your future was wasted, be it in respect to finding work or getting a recommendation from any party organization, not to mention that your files would forever remain in the records of the security services. This is a big part of Soviet history and has already been written by the victims of the NKVD and is now well established. It might lead you to think that most people were party members, but that was not the case. Out of a total population of two hundred million after the war, party membership represented a relatively small minority of seven million, but this minority had a hold on the entire country and every individual in it.

Enormous efforts were devoted to the training of cadres, recruited especially among the youth, wooed into the Pioneers from a very young age, and subsequently enrolled in the *Komsomols* during adolescence. Party members who could read and write were shunted toward night school for a period of four years. Obviously, those cho-sen met certain criteria, and only the most gifted were sent to study. This is how I found myself in evening classes in Vilnius after the war. We were taught basic subjects, like Russian, some Lithuanian, and last but not least Marxism-Leninism and party history. Russian geography and the geography of the Eastern countries was one of the fundamental subjects. We studied and studied Marx's *Capital* over and over again, as if it were the Bible; the twenty volumes of Lenin's *Complete Works*; and Stalin's twelve tomes. Among those graduates who finished these courses at the party school, a few were chosen to attend further classes. They were designated to benefit, again for four years, from the evening courses at the Marxist-Leninist Univer-sity that was in every Soviet republic. Once again I had the unbeliev-able luck of being selected. In spite of the propaganda, the lies, and the ideology, the eight years spent in the midst of this indoctrination brought me knowledge of economics, politics, and even philosophy. Naturally, only materialist philosophers were studied, and not all of them, either. All in all, having access to an education, however par-tial and biased, finding myself with people who knew about things of which I was ignorant, discussing with them subjects that had been unthinkable beforehand, led me to think for myself, to pose new questions, and, finally, to a fundamental self-reassessment.

At the end of the eight years of study, once we had our diplomas, and if we still had some energy and desire left, we were "free" to be sent for two more years, full-time, to Moscow University, where we would complete our advanced studies and become a state cadre. With four years in the army under my belt, and the eight years of studying that I had just completed, I felt absolutely no desire to keep it up. I had become an official party propagandist and was being sent into businesses to hold conferences, always after work. The subjects were economics, politics, or philosophy, which were sometimes com-bined into a simultaneous grand subject, but always dealt with in accordance with the party line.

Let's look at how Russification of the republics was organized from an economic point of view. Production was designed in such a way that no enterprise manufactured a complete item, be it a simple or sophisticated piece of production. No one had oversight over an entire part of the process and was independent of other sites of production. For example, machine parts were manufactured in various republics, preferably not those places where they could be assembled or sold, while the principal parts were almost routinely made in Russia. Given that, at the end of the day, the state was still the owner, this system was highly detrimental to the republics as a whole, because transportation costs increased the price of manufacturing without any rationale. Nothing about the system was innocent. The ultimate goal of organizing it this way was to make all of the republics dependent on the others and, ultimately, on Moscow. The well-known five-year plan, dictated by Moscow, forced the republics to meet a five-year deadline, although a number of plants were doing two and even three times what the directives called for by collectively applying the "Stakhanovist" system.[3] Here is where the deception began. When factory managers understood the political benefits that could be gained from lying about heroic levels of production, then falsification of production statistics became generalized. Everybody knew it, and everybody was turning a blind eye. While standing in line everywhere, in front of empty stores, there were plenty of reasons to question the official reality claiming we were living in an era of overproduction . . . according to the Stakhanovist mythology. A good worker who turned out twice what he had been assigned in his eight hours became the latest hero and ascended into the Stakhanovist pantheon. In companies where workers performed piecework, those workers who were the most productive got to the point where they earned twice what others did. But at what cost to the worker? The plan took nothing into account—neither supply nor demand, or the chances of selling and moving goods, to say nothing of the real needs of the population. Some enterprises manufactured goods that no one

3. Stakhanov was a model worker distinguished for his productivity and made a sacred legendary hero by Stalin.

had ever ordered and no one needed, or maybe at the other end of Russia. Yet it was written into the plan. One factory thousands of kilometers from Moscow was manufacturing nails, millions of nails, while on the other side of the country you couldn't find a store selling nails. I saw with my own eyes a wagon arrive with men's shoes that was loaded with left shoes only. The bureaucracy and the chaos cannot be described, and one day the whole system had to burst like a soap bubble, which is what finally happened. But despite how dishonest and crooked the system was, or precisely because it was so, no one could see it coming at the time. On the other hand, the great achievements of heavy industry were still making progress, but always at the expense of light industry meant for mass consumption. The human being counted for nothing. All energy was mobilized with a view to propaganda and the country's prestige, so we could "catch up with and surpass America."

Nobody could say we were starving, but a woman running a household had to rush from one store to another to know where the wolves were being thrown their food. In popular language, it was called *vibrasit*, throwing away. Once the correct store was unearthed, the lines would last for hours, and the goods would turn out not to be the ones you were expecting or anything you needed. If a shipment of ties came in, nevertheless a line would form for ties. The real tragedy of this economy was that no one took the slightest initiative to change a single thing, whatever that might be. Why bother, since you would still be paid in any case?

With the absence of a free agricultural market, the *kolkhoz*, the collective farm system, and the *sovkhoz*, the large model state farms that operated as sort of pilot specialized agricultural stations, failed in the same proportion. Forced to produce grain to feed not only big cities and towns but also the army, they were under such constraints that grain was always in short supply, and the state was forced to buy enormous quantities of agricultural products from abroad. Before the October Revolution, the Ukraine alone could feed all of Russia and still produce enough for export. It was known as the breadbasket of Europe.

Let's take a little time to look at things that functioned better than in the West. The health care system was free and enabled someone to be cared for at the hospital or clinic at no charge. Though medication was not free of charge, it was sold at a modest cost. Moreover, functionaries and workers were entitled to free medication and thermal or therapeutic cures, something referred to as *putiovka*, literally, "the road map." This privilege was granted by the unions, and workers with Stakhanovist status were the first to benefit from it. Schooling, in spite of the methods of indoctrination, was pretty well organized. Everyone was granted a free education, from primary school up to university. Doctors, engineers, and research scientists were all highly qualified. After their studies, each one found a job, even if it was poorly paid. A cobbler or tailor made more than a doctor or a professor. As far as housing went, nobody would sleep in the street; everyone had a roof over his head. Families were often required to share apartments, which created some severe proximity issues. The shared kitchen frequently caused a descent into open conflict. But in general, a single person was given a room, a couple always had one, and a big family used to live in two small ones. In the smaller towns that had not undergone shelling, and where the entire Jewish population had been exterminated, a family normally occupied a whole apartment. The cost of rent and electricity was also modest. I won't go so far as to say it was paradise, but from a strictly material viewpoint, neither was it hell. Obviously, there was a small minority who lived in luxury, the apparatchiks, cadres of the administration and the army. But workers didn't fear for their jobs, and employers couldn't throw you out on the street when you turned fifty. As paradoxical or even comical as it may seem, people were closer to one another and friendlier than in Western societies. You made friends easily and had fun without too much second-guessing. Work took up five days of the week, and in large enterprises there were two or three eight-hour shifts. No one worked on Saturday or Sunday.

The most difficult thing was to keep workers around for meetings after hours, scheduled once or twice per week and occasionally lasting for more than two hours. The subjects often addressed workplace discipline, the five-year plan, or the latest political question. Not all workers were in love with these meetings. A notable part of them was always looking for a way to escape this duty. The number of sick fathers, mothers, and children and funerals was never greater than when meetings were being held. There was an endless inventiveness to the excuses invoked, anything to go home. But there was no problem to which Communism would not find a solution. One simply had to lock the one and only factory's gate! There was a story that went around Vilnius. One day, a high-level party official was invited to a meeting. As his chauffeur-driven car pulled up to the factory, the apparatchik noticed some workers climbing over the wall. He stopped and asked the workers, "Why are you climbing the wall? Did you steal something? Did something happen at the factory?" The frightened workers answered, "We're honest workers. We've taken nothing, and the factory is not on fire." "So why are you climbing this wall?" "There's a meeting going on, and the gate is locked."

Managing the vocational school was getting more complicated by the day and, to tell the truth, becoming pretty perilous for me. Shortages were serious, and everything seemed to be lacking. And I do mean everything. Ration cards for basic necessities, while legal tender, were unavailable most of the time. Party members who were the recipients of coal deliveries would sometimes send their drivers to ask for foodstuffs. I daily felt like I was walking a tightrope and that one mistake could very well send me to the gulag after a stop at the local prison. The perversity of the system was such that from the moment you were arrested, not a single influential party cadre would acknowledge your existence, even though refusing a favor to any of these important people was absolutely out of the question. A lot of them, whom I didn't know from Adam or Eve, were looking to establish friendly ties with me for the sole purpose of obtaining something. My address seemed to be widely known throughout the city. Afraid as I was, this went on for almost three years until I got up the nerve to put an end to it and to leave this heaven-become-hell.

The director was one of those Russians dropped into the Lithuanian civilian administration out of the blue. He was not only a cultured man, an engineer, and a major authority on vocational schools, but, even more, he was a serious vodka drinker. And for that reason he would sometimes fail to appear in school for three consecutive days, if not longer. He always manifested a polite and even aristocratic refinement and the irreproachable courtesy of a person of breeding. In public he would never use informal terms of address, but when we drank together he did me the ultimate honor of being on a first-name basis and calling me Mikhail Itzikovitch. Having never gone to war himself, he respected me for my military decorations. Honorable man that he was, he was deeply annoyed by the interminable line of supplicants who had nothing to do with the school or the training, which is why he left that particular chore to me, sending them to me with a brief note, "Please provide depending on stocks," and preferring to get drunk somewhere, alone, and in a dignified manner. I understood what he meant and distributed according not to their look but to the length of their hand. He was sorry to see me leave, for practical reasons but also for reasons of friendship. He was a magnificent man who had long understood the system and had known how to protect his dignity.

My decision to leave this golden job was definitive and irrevocable. In the meantime, I was also asked to help in finding jobs, and I did so whenever I had the opportunity. I had obtained jobs at the school for one of my wife's sisters and for my cousin who was living with us and was an expert in precision mechanics. Through my new "acquaintances" in the ministries, I was successful in helping some army friends find work as well. As for me, I got out after three years before even finding new employment. In 1946 our son, Alexander, whom we called Sacha, was born, which invited me to envision the future in a different light. My personality had undergone a transformation, and I no longer needed the military uniform to flatter my self-esteem. It was merely for the parades on major holidays, but I no longer relished being in uniform. My situation had been excellent, and we lacked for nothing, which was precisely the reason I had to get out and work on myself, to conceive a fundamental change in my life so as to avoid any future responsibility for such a system. Obviously, there was no question of asking the party for a job, because "the bride was too beautiful." It would have been easy, but they would just have sent me to another factory in an equivalent position.

I ruminated on all of this anarchy and disorder. I couldn't say I was entirely innocent. Not only was I playing a risky game, implicating myself and my family, but I was also doing it mainly for people who weren't worth it, who had specialty stores at their disposal where they never had to wait in line. If I had given all of the goods to the poor, I would have been doing something useful. But the primary beneficiaries of my dealings were people in high places who could get along very well without me, by means legal or illegal, or even better by simple extortion. Gradually, I was growing more aware of the injustice, and I aspired to a more settled life. The risks of the war had been enough for me, and I came to reject this life, both dishonest and perilous, even though the whole society was gangrenous. As for the workers, they could be arrested for a trifle, being imprisoned for seven years just for being found leaving the factory with a spool of thread. A cadre occupying a high-level post could juggle truckloads without getting caught, because the system was corrupt and rotten. I told myself I no longer wanted honors or important jobs, no wreaths and flowers when I died. Without a doubt, this period caused me to offend people here and there, and these memories are still disturbing today and have left their marks. I had decided to become a *mentsh* again, an upright, no-tricks man, an honest worker who earned his living with his hands.

The Tailor and the Party

And so, after careful consideration, I resigned for good. The only trade that I really knew was that of a tailor. By working hard, my hope was to achieve calm and serenity. I found a job as a simple sewer and cutter of ladies' clothing in a *kombinat*, a group of tailoring workshops. It was piecework, and I worked very hard, earning a good living, though not as much as when I had access to everything for free at the vocational school. But now I was sleeping noticeably better, and above all my conscience was clear. I no longer had time to drink because I was working so hard. What use had I now to be a party member? To be a civilian and a party member could have had its benefits as well as a few drawbacks. When things go the party's way, it protects and defends you, helps you to find work and housing, training you for the future. It forces you to study continuously and to "progress politically." The party eats up all your available free time in various propaganda programs, something I had already experienced several times. In my *kombinat*, less than a tenth of the workers were party members, which is the reason they were pushing me to become union secretary, a nonpaying post that would absorb a lot of my time. Immediately, this consuming activity led to a decrease in take-home pay. I had to act decisively to come up with some prompt initiative if I was going to safeguard my free time and not sacrifice myself again for the sake of party propaganda. With my wife's approval, I enrolled in night school to study fashion design, for ladies only, attending classes from six to eight o'clock at night. We were also taught cutting. When I had completed the course, I spoke to the city committee of the party to get a job with my new skills in the city's only fashion house, renowned and respected for the quality of its work.

The factory, beautifully named Laisvé, or Liberty, already had twenty-two designers, mostly Jewish, and almost all fairly well along in years. By force of circumstance, the fashion designers were also the cutters. Every design was an original pattern handpicked from a catalog according to the whims of the client, who to distinguish themselves from the common lot would sometimes bring in magazines from Paris or America. These clients were wives of the *nomenklatura* or of army officers. Just like its name, Liberty, what was officially referred to as a factory did not correspond to reality. It was actually a fashion house with several departments: men's, women's coats and dresses, and children's. Children's clothes were produced in the same careful way, made to measure from a catalog. There was a middle-aged man at Laisvé who was a real expert in that area. On the first floor of this luxury elevator building, clients waited their turn to be received in an elegant salon surrounded by enormous changing rooms. If they were loyal to one designer, they sometimes had to patiently wait for a week because each of us had his own day. We, the designers, were always dressed to the nines, elegant and redolent with fragrance. These demanding, classy ladies aspiring to nobility, arriving in the company of their chauffeurs, could take hours to define the pattern they wanted, in addition to which came the choice of very fine-quality fabrics, linings, and accessories, provided by the house, and later on also a choice of furs.

Some less well-off people also had access to the fashion house, but rare were those who could really indulge themselves in crossing the threshold. A coat or a suit from the Laisvé factory was at least a month's salary for a worker. Those unfortunates without a title would grease the palms of the designers to speed up and "enhance" the service, which was always a little slower for them. Our communist country had a perfect pea-pod resemblance to a capitalist nation, or perhaps a banana republic.

This was the "factory" that I aspired to join as a designer. I, and everyone else in town, knew what the lifestyle of a designer was like. Officially, they earned more than government ministers. Before the advent of industrially produced clothing, designers were well respected in Russia. The party gave me a letter of recommendation addressed to the director, who was supposed to find a position for me. Again, I found a good buddy and no less of a good drinking companion in this new director. I was fresh out of school, without practice or experience, other than my years spent working as a tailor with the good specialists of Telz. But the letter was worth more than my training, and the director could not say no. Although no positions were immediately available, he did suggest that I wait until he organized a "brigade" of ten or twenty workers who would be taking orders from me. This personnel would have the job of sewing the designs I would create and to get them ready for the final fitting stage. Most of the designers working there were already well known in Vilnius, and a number of them were Jewish. As for me, I was still a young man, the youngest in the house, and I cannot really say that I was received with open arms.

That I was a party member and had come with the party's recommendation triggered in them a feeling of authentic terror, even panic. They all acquiesced without blinking, but certainly not out of respect for my craft or for me personally. There was no reason to hold it against anyone, and the idea of doing so never even crossed my mind. Yet this attitude lingered for a long time before it finally waned, although it never completely disappeared. Designers made an enormous amount of money, both officially and under the table. Tips, legally prohibited, sometimes came close to corruption. They must have thought that I had been sent by the party to spy on them or at least keep an eye on their business. Among the twenty-two designers, I was the only party member, and in addition my young age—I was about twenty-seven—precluded the possibility of friendly contact between us. Outwardly, everyone acted sociably with me, although I could sense quite a bit of hypocrisy in their behavior and discerned a concealed fear in their reactions from day one.

I have to add that the chief engineer, a Russian woman of about fifty, was not so happy seeing me "parachute dropped," recommended by the party. With all the other designers she acted like a partner, but she looked on me as one might a Martian. You could say she treated me like a bastard child more than a son. In her eyes I was far too young to have achieved the position I was entering. Given her administrative position, they all greased her palm, while from me she received nothing. Had I chosen to do likewise, as of course the system was transparent to me, she would have thought it was a trap. Our honeymoon was a cold one. Other than myself, there was only one other war veteran out of four hundred employees. The friend with whom I had attended design school was now in the men's department. He was the one to whom I ceded my position, with all the unpleasantness that came attached, when the time would come for me leave the USSR. I will speak more about that later.

In theory, these factors should have played out in my favor, but in practice I had neither enough experience nor acquaintance with the personnel and had the impression that the whole world was holding a grudge against me. I was like the boxer who was fighting his first fight. In other words, errors are committed in every job, and I was inevitably going to have my fair share. The best designer can always ruin a piece of clothing, and, as they say in Yiddish, an experienced doctor is honored to have a personal cemetery he supplies with occupants. Although my customers were not on their way to meet their maker, it did happen that some of them left dissatisfied or irritated, even going upstairs to complain to the chief engineer. They would complain that the style was not the one they had chosen, that it had been a failure, and, in the worst cases, that they wouldn't want it at any price. Don't forget that my customers were women, and what women! Not only of the upper ranks, most of them beautiful and thin but sometimes weighing more than 120 kilograms, quite short, and insisting on wearing styles that they saw in the newspapers. So whether a particular order went slightly wrong or not, the chief engineer was aching to jump at her chance. After all, who was to say what a failed design was exactly? Other designers had failures as well. A high percentage of the clothes that did not satisfy the original customers were put back on the shelves and sold as original creations to women who fought over them. The business never lost money on any of these garments. Everything depended on the perspective chosen. But regardless of these well-known facts of the trade, the chief engineer was inflexible and got busy mounting a case against me, even though in normal circumstances her deputy would have resolved the issue. She—the deputy—was a young Russian girl in her thirties, a very kind person who fulfilled her assignments from the workshops and had entirely another approach to her profession and to practical work. The chief engineer handled my case herself, "gently" telling me that another such incident would compel her to dismiss me from my position and demote me to the rank of an ordinary worker. She wasn't yet threatening to fire me.

This had been my rapport with her from the start, and when she advanced to the threat stage I became quite frightened. I had been there for only two weeks, and already she wanted my hide. I began to wonder why. The store was full of these so-called spoiled designs, and sales were still skyrocketing. One piece more or less wasn't a catastrophe. Clearly, she wanted rid of me like a fish bone caught in her throat that she couldn't swallow or spit out, and I was wondering how it would all end. What was my best response? I couldn't allow myself to continue being mistreated this way and focused on a way to handle the crisis. Even though this had been my first mistake, I was aware that my level of technical expertise fell short. Be that as it may, I told myself that I would proceed as though it were David versus Goliath. That may have been slightly exaggerated, but I had to assert my self-confidence and keep my spirits up. I felt that by doing nothing, I would soon be dead. The best defense being offense, the ex-soldier in me knew that to be true.

Normally, when a cutter or a designer started out, they gave him time to settle in and acquire experience. But in this pending crisis, fighting to remain a designer, my only weapon would be politics. I would obviously rather have avoided going down that road, but it was the only ground on which I could hope for an advantage. I had already been twice to the factory's party meetings and been greeted as a new friend. So I began to participate actively in the life of the party cell, which accounted for about thirty of the four hundred employees, including candidates for party membership. I got involved with the newsletter that was usually posted on a wall of the community room and wrote some articles for it. My adversary, Madame Chief Engineer, was looking out for the slightest error I might commit, but on my side I was also exerting my own faculties of observation. She was not a party member, and it was therefore easier for me to attack her on the basis of the kinds of labor relations she was creating within the firm. In one of the short articles I had written, I emphasized the point that she had never set foot in a workers' meeting, unseemly for a senior cadre whose duty was to participate in the political life of the factory and even its union events. In effect, she was someone who showed a lot of arrogance toward the workers and suffered from a very obvious feeling of superiority. Moreover, she never left her office to come down to the workshops. I was accumulating other little sins, which when added up made for a serious indictment. Since the verdict was not ensured, my greatest act of courage during the whole affair was signing my name to the article.

In hindsight I see a young twenty-seven-year-old Stalinist, well trained in the party line, fully indoctrinated, hardened to bureaucratic methods, and extremely combative. I had a family to feed. My time in war had taught me to fire at the enemy before the enemy fired at me. At the time, I still had all my medals and wore them on important occasions. In subsequent years, finally sobered up, lucid to the ways of the party and its politics, I would have seen the situation through an entirely different lens. I might even have taken the initiative of leaving before being chased out. But at the time my views were mostly still intact and fueled my combativeness. Hostilities were now joined on both sides. When she was informed by her employees that she had been publicly harangued by the young newcomer that I was, not only did she stop greeting me, but she fought with renewed energy and looked for any way to corner me. And though I was vigilant about not slipping up in my work, a perfect record in this profession is next to impossible, and naturally a customer finally ended up complaining. This occurrence was simply fate, just as we are born without knowing the date of our death—fortunately for us. Yet the injury was nothing more than a moral wound. Called into her office in the presence of the customer, I stood in front of the chief engineer, who began yelling insults at me, and I let her scream and gesticulate, absorbing the frontal assault. When she fell silent, I asked her what crime I had committed, and with my question left hanging, I saw that judgment had already been pronounced and there was no point in asking for clemency. She decided to immediately remove me from my post. But removing a party member from his job was not so simple. The gravity of the error had to be evaluated and a procedure followed.

The party meeting was scheduled fifteen days hence, and I used the time to defend myself. Once again I resorted to writing. The article was titled "Taking Revenge for Criticism" and denounced my enemy's lack of self-criticism. Beating one's breast *al chet*[1] was very fashionable in that period and in good alignment with the party program, called "self-criticism." Obstinate in her hostility, she preferred to continue going in the same direction, sullying a worker who had long had the party's confidence and who served the country, was wounded a number of times, and shed his blood on the front. Preparing my defense, I brought together evidence of my customers' satisfaction, often the wives of ministers or high-ranking officers and cadres whom I had known since the vocational school and had once helped.

It was clear that if I lost this position, not only would I never have any chance to work in the field again, but I would have trouble finding any other work, in any profession, in the Soviet Union, as your work record follows you everywhere and sometimes even precedes you. After an affair of this kind, your only recourse was to become

1. The *al chet* is the confession of sins pronounced ten times in the course of the Yom Kippur (Day of Atonement) service. Using Jewish religious concepts in paradoxical contexts is a feature of Yiddish humor and characteristic of Yiddish literature.

a night watchman or street sweeper. Assessments concerning your errors were indelible stigmas. My purpose here is also to paint a portrait of the system's distortions, and so I am lingering here on the vicissitudes of life in a society where government imposes arbitrary laws of survival and where corruption is rampant. The postwar context was quite simply more in my favor, but even so, you must understand that within the party there were periods when favor was shown toward party members and other periods when repression ruled. Why? You never knew why. A party member could do a lot of things in this system if he knew how to play the game. But the gamble was dangerous, and no one was invulnerable. In this risky game with shifting rules, Madame Chief Engineer played and lost, and she was transferred to another firm.

I did not utter a Kaddish to mourn her departure but, rather, breathed a little more freely.[2] Because of this whole affair, I had made a name in the business as well as in the party cell. It wasn't long before I was elected union secretary[3] and named a juror in the civil court, which sat in session twice a month. In the Soviet Union, all civil courts were made up of a judge and two jurors, each with a voice in the deliberations. At the moment of judgment, the verdict was announced on the spot after brief deliberations without a recess. Jurors had the right to interrupt the defense and even the prosecution, to ask questions, and to cross-examine the accused. If the two jurors disagreed with the punishment demanded by the prosecutor, their opinion took precedence. Most of the time, the verdict was subject to a negotiation with the judge. Judgments were severe, especially for petty thefts committed within businesses, though entire truckloads were driven out of the gates with real fake papers. Those who had committed major felonies were sometimes caught, but that kind of political account settling did not come under our court's jurisdiction.

2. Kaddish: Aramaic prayer said as part of the mourning rituals. See preceding note.

3. *Secretar fun der pro-farayn*: the professional union secretary.

My work in the factory was going very well. The engineer who was nice to me became the new chief engineer. To my great surprise, she ordered a coat from me with a complicated design that vouched for her recognition of my abilities. She chose a Parisian-style coat that had to look like it was cut from a single piece of material, bell shaped, with a hem three meters in circumference cut along the length of the fabric. This design still sold very well in Paris, when I emigrated a few years later and took the pattern with me. Unable to express myself in French, I could still draw and cut this design, which delighted the ladies and gave me a free pass to show up in the design houses. The engineer, who was tall and slender, wore it perfectly. Her husband was also an engineer but at another branch and, like so many husbands, came for the fittings and followed the progress of the work.

After a few months at the plant I was making a good living. I dressed elegantly, and several times a year I made for my wife the most beautiful outfits I came across. We were paid on production—in other words, per design. I was designing, cutting, and finishing between eighty and ninety patterns a month. Gradually, I was becoming so expert that I was managing to design the style directly on the material without preparing a pattern. Our clientele were often notable women figures or artists, coming from Moscow, Leningrad, and Minsk, because they had seen my designs being worn by others and absolutely wanted me to produce the models for them personally. The Russian artists called me Mikhail Itzikovitsh. I became an expert in working with fur, so prized by this select clientele who came to Vilnius for a few days while waiting for the completion of an order, which I finished during the nights, sometimes with Rose's help. At times the work was so overwhelming owing to their diva-like demands that my factory workers had to be conscripted. A fur coat brought me six thousand rubles, equivalent to what a worker made in a month. This was activity that was prohibited by law, but because of shortages in the supply of high-quality women's clothing, it was common practice in our line of work.

This is precisely the moment the party chose to send me to Marxist-Leninist University for four years, from six to ten at night, which tells you how full my days and nights had become. These universities were established in all the republics. Alone in my firm to have pursued higher political studies, I would from that point on become even more respected. At the time I was still a devoted Communist. When did I start to have doubts about my ideal, and when did my ideals begin to weaken?

I believed in a utopian ideal, and perhaps these beliefs never rose above the purely imaginary construction. I don't deny this possibility. Circumstances can change a person's opinions several times during his lifetime. Each one perceives morality, politics, and religion as a function of a sensibility shaped by the ups and downs of his history and its context. An individual's conscience is a factor of the times. A thing that had been absolutely true at one moment can lose all value in the next. There is no lack of examples.

In 1953 my wife gave birth to our little girl, Isabelle. It was less than fifteen days after the great Stalin died. Some weeks earlier, the affair of the "Jewish doctors," better known as the "Doctors' Plot" had begun. Jewish doctors were accused of poisoning members of the politburo. From one day to the next, their patients stopped seeing them. This orchestrated anti-Semitic state campaign was the final blow to my ideals and forced me to consult my own conscience. Later, Khrushchev's report to the Twentieth Communist Party Congress initiated a policy of de-Stalinization and peaceful coexistence with the capitalist countries. The report was studied in party cells, and I was in charge of introducing it in my cell. It revealed the existence of mass deportations, arbitrary executions, the liquidation of peasants, and accusations against Yiddish intellectuals and writers accused of "cosmopolitanism." But the report did not put an end to the anti-Semitic campaign, and new slogans appeared, recommending the "replacement of the party's upper echelons with national cadres," coded language for the elimination of the Jewish cadres, a process from which the local Russians parachuted into Vilna, who still did not speak the language, were strictly exempt—all remaining in their positions. In 1956, during the war between Israel and the Arab states, I was also sent into the factories and businesses to hold meetings denouncing the Israeli government. If this wasn't enough to make me rethink things, they were also sending us after work to destroy the old Jewish cemetery and exhume the bones in order to construct a large football stadium.[4] Anti-Semitism was getting stronger and stronger. I was obsessed with the situation and plunged into despair. Though not yet personally affected, I was distraught, and these events were compelling me to challenge everything about the system. In Yiddish we say that only asses are not capable of reflection and change. But a man who has the freedom of imagination and analysis has a duty to reexamine the way he sees things and the way he thinks, in a word his ideology.

I had a very good friend and comrade in the army, Dima. We had been in the same platoon. He was a Lithuanian-born Russian. After the war, he completed his studies at the most prestigious Marxist-Leninist University in Moscow, where he studied full-time for two years. On returning to Lithuania, he occupied high-level positions and was named regional party secretary. He was also a deputy in the Lithuanian Parliament as well as a member of the Supreme Soviet. He often came to visit from his province, where he was the big boss of everything. Each time he came to Vilnius, he came directly to the design factory and took me out for the afternoon. We enjoyed each other's company, giving ourselves a good time, drinking vodka and eating *zakuski*. In spite of the hotel that the government had reserved for him, we would go back to my home to make merry and stay overnight, joined by his chauffeur, who left the car in the courtyard.

---

4. Established in the fifteen century in the suburb of Šnipiškės, the oldest and largest Jewish cemetery (across the Neris River from the Gediminas Tower) was closed by the czarist authorities in 1831. It was destroyed by the Soviet authorities in 1949–50 during the construction of Žalgiris Stadium. Some graves of famous people, including that of the Vilna Gaon, were relocated to the new place from the old cemeteries before the destruction.

"Rozetshka," Dima would say to my wife, "why have you gotten so thin? Misha doesn't love you anymore?" In the morning, the chauffeur would accompany Rosa shopping at the marketplace, all dressed up, in the superb government automobile with room for ten, a Zim. The neighbors would wonder why Rosa was being taken away in a government car but finally got used to seeing the car "sleeping" in the courtyard.

Our two families were like one. Dima didn't have children and loved having fun with mine. We were so close that we went on vacation to his villa near Ponevezh. That's where Isabelle took her first baby steps at Easter. We were like kids ourselves, having fun. Nearby was a big lake where we would go night fishing, or so we said. Not the whole night anyway—a large part of it was dedicated to drinking and eating fish grilled on braziers that the fishermen stoked to keep warm. The reality was that we didn't always open our fishing rods, but when we got home in the morning our bags were full of fish the local fishermen supplied for us. Our wives did not think to ask where the fish came from and admired the good catch.

One day after a boozy meal, his chauffeur took us to go swimming in a river near the city where there was a place with a diving board. We didn't take all the precautions that are taken today before bathing, not to mention before diving. As we got out to dry ourselves in the sun, I began telling him what was tormenting me and the doubts I was harboring. My trust in him was absolute, and I knew he would never betray me. He observed me, hesitating, responding that he himself felt that way. My illegal departure from the USSR, a matter to which I will return later, was surely a fatal blow to his ascension up the ranks. For reasons of security, I was never able to say good-bye to Dima. Since our departure, I have never seen him again, and when I briefly returned to Lithuania in 1993, he was traveling.

Another friendship born at the end of the war had also meant a lot. When the war finally ended, the soldiers who no longer had exercises became bored. To avoid having them succumb to alcohol, the commandant found various ways to entertain the troops, organizing games within or between units. I was co-opted into our unit's football team, and we played a match against a team from another regiment. If you've been to football games, you know that this is a sport where you may launch a few whacks, but you have to be ready to take a few blows. Most of the time, feet or elbows are used for effect. It came to be that I gave a brutal kick to the leg of the opposing team's player. It wasn't deliberate, but what a cannon shot! Willful or not, it was serious, and the player had to be taken off on a stretcher. During the game, you don't pay attention to the injured, don't look closely at who it is, content to get them off the field and not unhappy playing eleven against the remaining ten, hoping to win the game. This time we lost; they were way better than we were. After the game I went searching for the injured player to apologize. We began to chat, and I asked him in Russian where he was from. "I'm from Gargždai, and my last name is Ackerman," he told me. I exclaimed that I too was from Gargždai and that my grandmother was an Ackerman; her name was Tsivia. He was so surprised that he forgot all about his pain and, almost laughing, forgave me, shouting, "Your grandmother was my grandfather's sister," which is how we became acquainted, Eli and I.

Since I was not all that sure about this version of our story, I wrote a letter to my cousin who now lives in Israel and asked him what he remembered about this episode. Since he failed to reply, I became impatient. Failing to receive an answer, doubts have taken hold of this story of our friendship. Perhaps my memory was faulty and I had in fact met him earlier on, since, after all, we were in the same infantry division. Yet, prior to writing my memoir, I had met this same cousin nearly a dozen times on my trips to Israel, without ever raising this question.

In the aftermath of the war, having both lost our families, we became very close. Like two real brothers, we were bonded by a reciprocal affection. I was demobilized before him and already back in civilian life, working at the vocational school and living in a big apartment. I suggested that until such time as he got married, he come to live with us like a member of the family. I got him work in the school where he taught precision mechanics, his profession. He stayed with us for a year. Our friendship endures today, tossed on the waves of emigration and the vagaries of our lives. The first time we met in Israel after being apart for twenty-five years, my wife and I traveled from Netanya to Rishon Lezion by taxi. We were so nervous that we forgot the enormous bouquet of flowers that the driver had placed in the trunk. The taxi and the flowers waited for us, but when we were heading back several hours later, the flowers remained abandoned forever in the car.

I had trouble recognizing Eli when I finally saw him. He had aged a great deal, moved around with difficulty, and seemed to have lost his zeal. He told me later on that he had found me very changed also and absolutely had not imagined me as I was. This anecdote reminded me of a play where a married woman, a mother and already a grandmother, wrestles with the memories of her youth when she was the lover of a young man, Kostia. During her entire life, this love had fueled her imagination. She spoke unceasingly about him as an icon, a kind and loving man. She lived with this illusion and at the slightest opportunity never failed to remind everyone of his exquisite manners. Over time, her husband, children, and friends all became used to hearing her extol Kostia's virtues. One fine day, she got a letter from Kostia, who intended to visit at last, after so many years of longing. The woman turned her house upside down, moved the furniture around, and dressed herself in flaming new clothes, as though she were getting married, and settled down, impatiently awaiting his arrival. The doorbell rings. She runs to open the door, and Kostia is standing there. When she sees him, she stands there dumbfounded. In front of her is an old, barely recognizable man who shuffles rather than walks. Only then does she sense all her dreams collapsing like a house of cards. Likewise, this reacquaintance with Eli after twenty-five years left us with a mutual feeling of loss. Our youth, our friendship, our vitality, what you see on the outside, had all departed with the times. In Yiddish we say *alte libe zhavert nisht*, old love doesn't go rusty. So what was left? Well, a dampened love that we had given another chance. We both understood that we were no longer young, that we were tied to families we had started in different countries, and that what was in the past would either separate us or bring us together again. In the course of time and over my trips to Israel, we did rebuild our relationship and became close without ever rediscovering the symbiosis of our youth. Not even a good kick could bring back the joy Eli had once felt when he lay there injured and learned I was his cousin. All things considered, our friendship had survived, but we had to give it another place in our lives. The only thing we could do was to adjust to the situation and accept the passing of time that had transformed us into men of a different era.

My cousin's letter finally arrived after a few months. From the two versions of our first encounter that I have written, Eli confirmed the first and most spontaneous recollections that I narrated here.

My Father, My Wife, and My Star

Life in Vilnius ran its course. We decided to buy a car, something pretty rare back in those days. We first had to register our names on a waiting list and, when our turn came, pay in cash, take the train to Moscow, and return to Vilnius with the car. Simplicity itself, right? Be that as it may, from a material standpoint, we lacked for nothing. Rosa never needed to go out to work and even had help from a live-in maid.

Let me tell you how I met my father again, a father who no longer occupied any of my thoughts and was hardly more than virtual, as he was physically gone for more than twenty years. This is how it happened. The rabbi of Vilna, the one who had performed our religious ceremony in the last synagogue left standing in the city, had left for America.[1] It was impossible to leave the USSR as a tourist or immigrant at the time. One had to come up with the right illegal combination—for example, as a Polish national, you could go back to Poland because there was an agreement between the USSR and Poland that gave former citizens the right to return to their homeland. There had always been a lot of Poles in Vilnius because the city had changed hands so often; they in fact formed the majority of the population until 1938. This was the route the rabbi and many

1. Reb Aizik Ausband, who had become the husband of Chaya Bloch, one of the three daughters of the rabbinical family Bloch, in Telz, who survived the Holocaust. One daughter also survived in Israel: http://batkamaat.org/?page_id=3538. See also note 1 in the chapter "Return to Life—L'chaim."

others had followed to get to Warsaw. From there, emigration was a little easier. His efforts were crowned with success, and he got his visa for Paris. In Paris he went to a community meeting designed to put newly arrived immigrants in touch with Jewish Parisians who were still looking for information about their families. By that time, people were no longer hoping to find survivors, but my father wanted to remarry and had no certainty about the fate of his family, his wife in particular. According to my father, by chance alone, he was within hearing distance of a man recounting in Yiddish to the community center worker that he had arrived from Vilna, where he had been a rabbi. On hearing this, my father bounded up to the man: "You said Vilne? I was born there and lived in Lithuania. My name is Rozenbaumas." "Rozenbaumas? Well, I was the Vilner rabbi and celebrated the marriage of Moishe Rozenbaumas in Vilne." And so my father learned he had a son who had survived. So, precisely because we had celebrated a religious marriage, he managed to get our address through the community. His first letter arrived in 1948 or the beginning of 1949,[2] and we rejoiced with all our hearts, truly, even if I had never taken any steps to search for him. In the letter, besides expressing to us how happy the news of our existence made him, he was letting us know that he was rich, an advertisement I could have done without because letters were carefully read by the NKVD's "letter service." This time, I'd been lucky. The letter had fallen into the hands of a friend who taught me to be careful in these matters. Since I was an active Communist, this type of statement could have been even more life threatening in my case. My father concluded his missive by declaring he already wanted to see all of us in Paris.

At the time, I did not envision any future other than in the Soviet Union. We exchanged scarce but regular letters, and he sent

2. The Yiddish text says 1953 or 1954. Moishe may have corrected this date when he worked with his daughter (the editor of the English version) on the French version. The early date is more plausible, as it is said that the correspondence was interrupted for security reasons and resumed later.

us clothing packages and later, according to my daughter, enormous bars of Poulain chocolate, with its trademark foal gamboling on golden cream paper, took up the length of a suitcase. In my opinion those bars were of normal size. Early on we received a scrap of paper in an envelope, a note apparently written in my father's handwriting, asking us to go to Warsaw in order to meet someone who supposedly knew how to get us to Paris. It was both very beautiful and very naive. For a party member, it provided food for thought before it could be acted upon. My immediate reaction and interior voice were distrustful, telling me this could only be a setup by the NKVD secret services. Obeying the impulse of such a plan, a fool could indeed leave without a visa, but he would be going much farther than Warsaw, all the way to Siberia, in fact. I never answered the note, acting as if I had never received it and for a while even stopped writing to my father. Time flew by, and a lot of Poles, Jews especially, took advantage of their right to leave for Poland. Vilna did belong to Poland in the interwar, and the two Communist regimes had signed an agreement to let the Poles go back to their country. Others who weren't Polish were putting everything on the line by taking the risk of traveling as a group aboard a truck to the Lithuanian-Polish border. Aboard one such truck was a girl I knew from my last tailor workshop in Telz, a beauty, and also an Auschwitz survivor.[3] Without warning, the border guards opened fire on the truck, and many were wounded. She was the only one killed. The others, it goes without saying, ended up in Siberia.

Many friends around us, who really were Polish, had already managed to leave. My wife tried to convince me that we too had to try to get to Poland, but neither she nor I had been born there, and I

3. See http://batkamaat.org/?p=1499. This young woman was Dvoyre Bod, whom Moishe mentions briefly in the chapter "*Der broyt geber*, the Breadwinner," who was the object of his secret inclination. The editor of the present book interviewed her sister Mina Bod in July 2008. She confirmed the information given by Rosa and Moishe Rozenbaumas. Dvoyre was killed trying to escape in the direction of Poland.

wondered how to skirt the quandary of our nationality. Though we might be successful in procuring false documents, what would be our fate if we failed? They would most likely come for us. I would have rather lived in Vilnius than among polar bears. But Rosa insisted and gave me no pause. You haven't seen your father for almost twenty-five years, she would say, and we have to take the risk. Being a woman and being religious, Rosa was probably more sensitive to myriad bad omens clearly perceptible from the regime and from society. Just before Rosh Hashanah, the Jewish New Year, she assured me that this year, if I fasted on Yom Kippur, God would come to help me and I would see my father again the following year. She was constantly entering the fray, *eyn breyre*, no choice, we used to say. Rosa exactly predicted the sequence of events that unfolded. As a first step, I began by believing in my wife . . . After all, I had already fasted a lot in my life, just maybe not for the same motivations. I had been hungry more than one time in my childhood and later during the war, and, after all, one day more or less wouldn't kill me. I embraced my destiny wholeheartedly and started to foresee the possibility of our departure. And you really had to believe in something to initiate the process.

It wasn't that easy finding the perfect person on whose door to knock, asking for no less than fabricating false papers. To get it right on the first try especially was a neat trick, because there would be no second chances. One of my acquaintances, my secretary at the vocational school, was now working for a notary who turned out to have been in my division, was Jewish, but was not a party member. He was the one who gave me the name of the appropriate person and made it clear that I should anticipate paying a tidy round figure. It was written that chance was smiling on me throughout this whole affair. The person in question turned out to be a woman, a client of mine who had ordered an elegant model in the past and the daughter of a Russian general. And luck had brought me across the paths of these three people, had arranged things in such a way that all three of them were disposed to help me, and none was prone to betraying me, all for reasons that were their very own.

When I knocked on the general's daughter's door and told her the reason for my visit, she was friendly and led me to understand that these affairs were very difficult and risky but . . . This "but" was the little space signaling she was ready to take the risk and that a trade could take place. I understood what she wanted and acceded to her demand. The sum represented roughly the going price of two cars. Let's say something like a large purchase. Because imagine that in order to obtain a fake birth certificate, it would be necessary to falsify the birth registry itself, in such a way as to create a blank where a new name could be introduced over the old one. When we received the first forged document from her, which certified Rosa's birth in Poland, we used it to apply to the state for an actual passport. No citizen was in possession of a passport document in the USSR, which was delivered to individuals only in case of a definitive departure from the country. Ours arrived before long.

We began selling furniture and whatever else had a value. Please understand that in the Soviet Union, everything can be sold, new or used, mother or father. It had to be done quickly; the clock was ticking, and the ground was burning under our feet. We had to deal with the question of our apartment and succeeded in having one half registered in the name of Rosa's sister Golda. To get the necessary authorization to take the car out of the country, I had to go to Moscow and on the same trip acquired some items that could not be found easily in Vilnius, notably a few gold watches that were easy to transport. It may seem paradoxical, even bizarre, but I even bought a big refrigerator. How naïve we were.

In Moscow I had the honor of staying in the same hotel as Simone Signoret and Yves Montand during their visit in December 1956.[4]

---

4. Simone Signoret (1921–85) and Yves Montand (1921–91) were French actors and a couple, extremely popular for their filmography but also for their involvement in left-wing political causes, and later against authoritarian regimes. Simone Signoret has an article in the Jewish Women's Archive: https://jwa.org/encyclope dia/article/signoret-simone. See Costa-Gavras's films Z and The Confession. The Confession is the real-life story of Artur London, a loyal Communist who certified

They were hugely popular in the USSR, and in the lobby of the hotel, a large crowd waited for them, eager to get their autographs.

As soon as I returned to Vilnius, I had to take care of certain matters pertaining to work. In the USSR, someone who is working is forced to "voluntarily" underwrite a loan to the state of at least one month's salary. Because a Communist has to set a good example, I had underwritten one for two months every year. So the state owed me two months of salary plus eleven years of interest. The bank gave me the money in a small suitcase full of rubles that certainly wasn't worth very much, but, hey, it was a suitcase all the same. Items that in Russia were overpriced did not necessarily have any value in the West. Other than in consignment shops, it wasn't easy to purchase valuable merchandise. We spent as many rubles as we could, and among the other things we bought was a beautiful professional accordion.

Travel fever was getting to us, fear was eating at us, and the waiting seemed interminable. In reality, things were moving along pretty quickly. I was the one who was most afraid. When I risked my life during the war, I was alone and didn't have a family, but now things were quite different. I had a wife and two children. Under the same circumstances, an ordinary citizen who was caught and arrested

---

his credentials by serving with the International Brigade in Spain and with the Communist anti-Nazi underground in France and by a long term in a Nazi concentration camp. In 1949 London returned to his native Czechoslovakia from France to become undersecretary for foreign affairs in the Communist government of President Klement Gottwald. Two years later, along with thirteen other leading Czech Communists (eleven of whom were Jewish), London was arrested for treason and espionage and found guilty in what became known as the "Slansky trial." The Slansky trial, named for the secretary-general of the Czech Communist Party, who was also a defendant, was one of the last major gasps of the Stalinist purges that began with the Moscow trials in the 1930s. All of the Slansky defendants were found guilty, and all but three, including Artur London, were executed. London lived not only to see the defendants rehabilitated and to write his book but also to return to Czechoslovakia on the day in August 1968 when Soviet troops invaded his country to end the short Czech Spring.

would get several years in prison. For someone like me, it was even more serious. For entire nights I couldn't get myself to sleep. I wasn't shaving and was neglecting my appearance. In winter I was usually seen in a beautiful overcoat and an astrakhan gray hat, but that year I had become unrecognizable, my work no longer held any interest for me, and people around me thought I was sick. Yet there were still two serious problems I had to resolve. The first issue was easier, the need to find a designer who would agree to take over the work I had yet to finish. Hundreds of pieces awaited assembly, and patterns that were cut but incomplete were still hanging up. It was very sought-after work, and there was no shortage of candidates. Even so, it had to be someone trustworthy. I asked my army friend with whom I had studied at the school for design if he wanted to take over the job at the fabric department where he was working as a simple worker in the men's department. I was leaving him with a very good job that earned a lot of money, but there was a matching poison pill, which was the second problem that needed resolution. He would be the one that had to take my party membership card, which in Russia was called the "party ticket," down to the party committee.

Of all blunders I made, this one was the biggest and most grievous. Reason always comes too late. I was extremely anxious, and fear is a phenomenon that deprives you of all judgment. I had been scared to go and drop off my party membership card myself. Writing this today, I realize how stupid you can end up from indoctrination. Obviously, I didn't need to bring the card anywhere, or send it, or take it with me. I could have simply discarded it. Someone living in a free country cannot comprehend a tragicomedy of this nature or understand how I could have come so close to exposing myself and my wife, and my children, for no purpose whatsoever, and, down the line, placing my friend in danger as well. Now that I am a free man, I am able to ponder thus and such different options, to analyze why I should have pursued another course. In the fever of the moment, I had chosen the worst, most foolish, one.

So then my friend, who was to replace me at work, was to take my card to the regional party committee, but only after we had departed and arrived in Warsaw. I speculated Gomulka, who was then in power in Poland, had deteriorating relations with Moscow, so even if they arrested us at the request of the Russians, the Polish authorities would not get any benefit from handing us over to the NKVD and sending us back to Lithuania. As things turned out, from the moment my friend returned the card, a scandal erupted. The regional committee, through the NKVD, began an investigation, interrogating my friend, demanding to know how a party member like him had been able to get the card of another member without coming in to denounce him before he could leave the country. It caused him, I have to face it, a lot of trouble and really shook him up. He played innocent, pretending that he didn't know he didn't have the right to do what he did. His medals did the rest. I saw him again twenty years later in Israel, where he had emigrated, and a thousand times asked his forgiveness for having gotten him mixed up in this story. In the end, the main and most comforting thing was that he too had gotten out, safe and sound. Although he was able to keep my former job, the Inquisition-like investigation was not to end soon. The NKVD conducted a detailed inquiry to learn how I was able to procure the perfectly executed counterfeit passport. They were looking for culprits.

But let's get back to our departure from Lithuania. We bought plane tickets for Warsaw. I had already sent the car by train. We had acquired a dozen suitcases. Everything we couldn't sell we distributed within the family. We then went around the city to say our good-byes to friends and relatives who would be as discrete as we were and to the airport, where the close family gathered to bid farewell. Rosa alone had a large family, her mother with six sisters and a brother, her uncle and her aunt and their five children, not to mention quite a few cousins and second cousins who were there. If one wanted discretion, then this was as discrete as possible. When we arrived at the airport, we still had to put our names on the waiting list of Poles emigrating to Warsaw. The people assembled there, who had already been in the waiting room for several days, were, in contrast to us, completely legal. According to what I heard later from people arriving in Warsaw after us, our escape had been the first case of leaving with documents that were bogus. There was no way we could allow ourselves the luxury of waiting several days for our turn to leave. Any further delay would have been much too dangerous. It was for us a matter of life or death.

Our departure fell on December 31, 1956, when everyone was preparing to celebrate the new year. Airport staff was reduced to a minimum. What did I do in such a touch-and-go situation? I began running through the airport to see if there was anyone I knew. Once again luck was smiling on me. I ran into a high-ranking general who used to accompany his wife on her visits to the design shop for her orders. As I've told you already, anything could be bought in Russia, so without going into details, I told him we were in a real hurry and slid an envelope into his hands that corresponded to six months of his salary. Appreciating its thickness, he advised us on how to proceed and recommended above all that we not put our names on the departure list. He knew that we would not be able to leave that day and helped us get a room that was designated for foreign tourists in transit. He promised that the next day, a cargo plane would be stopping to refuel, and we would be driven with our baggage through a service entrance, then we could board, while he would make arrangements with the captain. The night seemed interminable. With fear gnawing at us, neither Rosa nor I could think of sleeping. With every noise, we thought they were coming for us.

The contact person arrived as promised, very early in the morning. However, he could not help us avoid customs. So with porters, our ten suitcases and enormous refrigerator were sent directly to customs. A functionary did a very detailed inspection, systemically unpacking and searching each piece. Rosa was not only very beautiful but elegant, with a peerless cool. Her pockets were bulging with gold Russian watches and matching gold bracelets. Each time she was told to repack a piece of luggage and close it, she would surreptitiously slip one or two of the watches and bracelets in. A few other valuable objects went the same route. The relatives who had accompanied us the previous evening were still there or came back at dawn.

Not one was missing, and a lot of tears were shed. I was the first one sneaking out with real false papers. Those who surrounded us knew under what conditions we were leaving and trembled for us.

At last, we were all aboard the plane, with the children, the innumerable bags, and the large refrigerator. The moments that followed were the longest of our lives, a never-ending suspended time. It seemed like the plane would never take off. When it did finally climb into the sky, and was finally flying, we could breathe again. But we remained anxious and forlorn. The flight didn't take very long. We had the address of a woman in Wroclaw[5] who would welcome us, but we didn't know how far it was from Warsaw. In fact, we had to rent a truck to go the extra four hundred kilometers to the indicated address. There we were greeted by a childless couple who rented us a room in their house. It was another mistake, because our applications could be made only in Warsaw. We had saved enough money to be able to stay in Warsaw's best hotel for a year, but it seemed like we were at the other end of Poland. Every time we needed to visit the Israeli embassy in Warsaw, we took a small commuter plane that shook so much we got sick. We never took the children with us, and if anything were to happen to us we would be leaving two orphans behind. Poland was then the only Eastern Bloc country to have relations with Israel, and getting a visa for Israel was the only way you could leave Poland. We reestablished telephone contact with my father in Paris. Fearing that the Poles might close the borders, he advised us to drop everything and leave as quickly as possible. But things were not that simple; there was no possibility of leaving directly for Paris. The only open door was to Israel.

This was also a long wait. Having the time to think, after a month in Wroclaw it became clear that we should move to Warsaw.

---

5. A small booklet belonging to Rosa has, as a first entry in its address book (beginning from the Hebrew-Yiddish side, from right to left), the name and address of a man in Wroclaw, Ul. Barlickiego 28/6 Polska. On the page facing this address were written the Hebrew dates of commemoration for the Jews from Telz.

So we sold our things, including the car, and went to Warsaw, where we rented a room in either the Hotel Central or the Europa, I can't remember which, across from the city's tallest building, the House of Culture, a fifty-story skyscraper. We sold everything we didn't need to acquire enough zlotys, the Polish currency, to pay our expenses. We stayed there two months and a total of three in Poland, which may not seem a very long time, but enough to receive the visits of several acquaintances arriving from Vilnius through the regular line. We learned from them the rumors going around about our affair in Lithuania. The scandal revolved especially about the ridiculous business with my party card. To the NKVD, it was a crime. In Vilna, because imaginations were running wild, everyone was talking, but no one told the same version, adding to the story as the whim occurred. We were told they were still looking for us or, better yet, that we had already been arrested. These widely disseminated hearsay and false reports made our hearts beat faster than usual.

These threats cast shadows on our spirits, and we no longer felt much like going out or having fun. The only pleasure I was able to allow myself was, several times a week, the steam baths with my son. I already knew the Russian steam baths and felt at home. We swam in the pool first and then climbed the bleachers, where we would lash ourselves with branches until our bodies turned a nice beet red. The lashing was strong enough that branches lost their leaves. When we got tired, we went and rested at the bar, or at a table laid out with *zakuskis*, and ordered a vodka or two. The most delicate dish was chicken neck stuffed with grated potatoes. Once we felt revived again, we went back to the steam-bath bleachers, and this continued until one was either too drunk or too exhausted. After several such drills, my son and I would return to the hotel. Under the circumstances, and knowing it was a pleasant distraction for my son, these times represented the few very agreeable hours that relaxed me and allowed me to forget the pressure.

The steam bath was also a place that allowed you to meet people and talk more freely on various subjects. Especially after a few drinks, tongues were loosened. Unfortunately, after the war there

were not many Jews left in Warsaw, where Jewish life had once bubbled over. At the bath, the majority of the customers were Jewish.
Those coming now were passing through on their way to other countries. I gleaned news from every corner of Lithuania and even from
other parts of the USSR. Some people had left Russia for Poland
simply because life was easier there, for even though economic conditions were difficult, they were still less stringent than in Moscow. I
heard a humorous anecdote in Warsaw, and naturally the baths were
the place to catch or pass on such stories. Two Jews, Berl and Yankl,
meet each other on the bleachers of the steam bath, and Berl goes up
to the fifth level, where it is very hot. A moment goes by, and he says
to Yankl, "You know, Yankl, I don't feel very well." Yankl, naturally,
answers with a question: "Have you recently seen anyone who is
feeling well?" Another few minutes pass, and Berl starts to complain
again. "You know, Yankl, I am feeling very bad. I can't take any
more." Again Yankl responds that he is also feeling very bad. After
several more complaints go unanswered, Berl passes out at the foot
of the steps, and a flabbergasted Yankl yells at him: "Berl, you should
have told me you weren't feeling well . . ."

The four of us went to visit the site of the ghetto that the Germans had liquidated and torched. After the Jewish fighters rose up
for their freedom, all that was left was an area of flaming ruins. We
also visited other Jewish neighborhoods, where we met only a few
elderly people haunting the tiny community, and stayed at the head-
quarters of the Kehilah.[6] There was a kosher restaurant where you
could get a good meal for a modest sum, and for the needy, or people
in difficulty, the meal was free.

Every second day we headed to the Israeli embassy to ask how
far our paperwork had advanced and each time received the same
answer. But we were relentless and increased the number of our visits. There were any number of Rosenbaums in Warsaw, and several
times we rejoiced before our hopes were dashed. One fine day, we

---

6. Kehilah: the Jewish community and its organization.

didn't yet have the time to declare our identity to the clerk whom we had gotten to know, when he yelled to my wife, "Madame, ir zayt shoyn fartik!" (Your papers are ready!). But this turned out to be wrong again. Soon enough, however, our visas did arrive in the name of Rozenbaumas, a name rare enough that this time we knew it was for real.

Isabelle turned four in Warsaw on March 19, 1957. A few days later, toward the end of March, we were assembled into groups, each one designed to fill one railroad car. The entire train was filled with Jews who were leaving, via Vienna, for the land of Israel. The noise was considerable and the celebration only more so, an indescribable hoopla and mayhem. There was such a motley assembly of people who seemed to have come from a bygone era, so quaint and olden was their appearance. You might have thought you were in the nineteenth century. There were old people bent over in two, widows and widowers, couples with children of every age, little babies in the arms of their mothers, and older ones of marrying age.

The train moved off as our hearts smashed to pieces, not that we were not glad to leave, but the toxic clouds of fear darkened our anticipated joy. We were heading toward Czechoslovakia, at the time the most pro-Soviet of the so-called independent countries that had been liberated by the Red Army. In reality, the people of the Eastern Bloc countries were suffering under Moscow's boot. The Budapest uprising of 1956 had been the first sign of rebellion. Czechoslovakia, Moscow's pet student, still zealously applied all the *ukazes*, or dictates, of Soviet power. At the border, Polish customs acted very crudely and showed open hostility toward the Jewish train. We were not inspected on the Czech side. However, as we approached Austria, the train came to a halt at a little village. Two men dressed from head to toe in black leather overcoats and hats, the spitting image of NKVD agents, came up to us. We then really believed that the Russians would take us off the train. In fact, though they were indeed NKVD officers, they were there only for a general inspection of the convoy. Fortunately, this fright was needless. This was the last alarm we experienced.

Once across the Austrian frontier, we heaved an enormous sigh of relief and truly began to breathe like free men. Today I have to sleep with a breathing apparatus because of a case of sleep apnea. Can I consider myself a free man? Well, life under a Communist regime has a lot in common with being dependent on a machine for breath, but at least I can remove the mask when I want to. We were on our way to Vienna, where we would get off the train to meet my father and his wife. They were to come from Paris to welcome us and get acquainted.

When he had learned that my mother had been murdered by the Lithuanians, my father remarried in 1946. Odette, his wife, had saved his life during the war by getting him out of prison and then hiding him. I had lost my mother and my three brothers who had shared her fate, and so in my father, my stepmother, and their little girl, I was once again finding a family. My half sister, Françoise, was nine years old, but she wasn't with them then. When I first met her she represented, because of my lost brothers, more than a sister to me, and she was about the same age as the youngest of them when he died. Eli was only ten when we had been separated. For me, Françoise became a very sweet little sister, a precious gift from above. I will return to this relationship that was to mean so much to me.

When we arrived in Vienna, my childhood feelings toward my father resurfaced. Naturally, during the first few years after he left, there had been a lot, perhaps excessive amounts, of resentment. But as time passed, frustration dulled. I still had grievances toward him, but I had become both more reasonable and more responsible. I had seen so many terrible things throughout the war. After the tragedy that had annihilated our people and my family, my point of view had significantly changed. Not because I had forgiven everything, but because after being apart for twenty-seven years, our meeting generated a little space for joy and solace in my heart. It wasn't a generous or full pardon, for the good reason that at the very sight of my father, the reminiscences of the past stubbornly emerged. In spite of myself, his very presence provoked a flood of painful memories, which for so long I had made every effort to deter. I never uttered a word of blame toward him, however. What good would it do? I dealt with the situation as I found it.

As for my wife and children, they were very happy. My son, Sacha, spoke Yiddish, but Isabelle, as blonde as a Pole and very sharp for her four years of age, at that point spoke only Russian. Ten-year-old Sacha entertained long conversations with his grandfather, which was not the case with me. But no one could speak French with Odette. An accordion for Sacha and a doll as tall as she was for Isabelle were the gifts my father brought for the kids. As it happens, we always called Isabelle by her nickname, Kukelke, which means precisely "little doll" in a Yiddishized Russian.

Before leaving Vilna we had already acquired a professional accordion, a beautiful instrument. As a result, we now found ourselves with two accordions, despite the fact that Sacha had learned piano (and even violin to begin with). We could have formed an orchestra, but Sacha did not continue with his music.

After the first wave of joy, we had to board another train. This new convoy, made up exactly the same way, had to get us to Naples. A little reorganizing was needed to make space for Odette and my father in our compartment. The route was long, and the noise of the train still accompanied us, but from now on it was another journey. The tumult created by these Jewish families was, *keyn eyn hore*, may the evil eye be kept far away, considerable. Nevertheless, my father and I managed to find a little corner in the corridor for a face-to-face talk away from the family. We ended up speaking without really saying anything, without dealing with the problems that were close to my heart. The train lumbered on its way to Naples, where all the immigrants were supposed to embark on a ship to Israel. All the while gazing at the magnificent countryside, my father had time to deepen his thoughts about my future and the road I would take. He didn't know how to handle this. Finally making up his mind, he took out a thousand dollars from his pocket. "Listen, Moishe," he said to me, "here's a thousand dollars to get started in Israel." I don't know whether that had been his plan when he left Paris or if maybe the flame of Zionism inside of him had suddenly rekindled. Whatever the reason, I was taken by surprise by this never-expressed political idealism, for which I was totally unprepared. I had hardly just renounced my belief in Marxism, and here already I was expected to embrace the fixed idea of Zionism. And for that it was much too early.

First, I thanked him for the money, which I immediately returned, pointing out that his gesture was completely unrelated to the message contained in his letters, in which he wrote to us that we should come and that he was sufficiently well off to see to the family's needs. I asked him which family he meant. He had even called us in Poland, telling us to leave everything, to forget our belongings behind and meet him in France as soon as possible. My father had a little trouble continuing the conversation. After a few moments of thought, and seeing that his gesture had been badly received, he reconsidered. "If you don't want to go to Israel, I'm going to try to get you papers so you can come to France." There had never been any question between him and me that we would go to Israel. I had already tackled this question of patriotism. Having been a patriot in the USSR, I wasn't overly interested in being one anywhere else. On that point, our discussion ended. Nobody knew about our talk. The rest of the trip unfolded without confrontation but also without coming any closer together, taking several more days. Time went by slowly. We spoke neither of the past nor of the future. Our comments related to banal things, concrete things, the view, the meals, sleep.

Apart from the personal problems, for us the trip was a great novelty. At the time we had never experienced anything like it. No, absolutely nothing like it. Where we came from in Lithuania, a country of forests, lakes, and flowing streams, hills don't offer a relief higher than a few hundred meters, if that. And here we were at the end of March, crossing the majestic, snow-covered Alps, which took our breath away. There was no shortage of snow in Lithuania. Only once it reached to your waist did you think there was too much of it. But this was our first encounter with mountains, and we were filled with wonder at their splendor.

And what can be said about Italy, which we were descending north to south in springtime, the southern landscapes, the buildings painted pink and green, the villas, the roads with their to us so well-maintained appearance, even in the smallest villages we glimpsed from the train. And the flowers, everywhere flowers. We were still in a dream state where everything was novel. Never before in our lives had we seen anything like it. We had just landed on another planet. I had crisscrossed Russia from one end to the other, and it is a magnificent country. But it is wild and poor. Italy is densely urbanized, but each house, each building, displays elements of style and refinement, a care and a taste that speak to its age-old culture. We were carried away, elated, euphoric as though inebriated. Even today, if you go to Italy after a trip to the Eastern Bloc, Italy impresses you as a wealthy country. What we were seeing inflamed my imagination and contributed to strengthening my hopes. Was our life going to resemble what we saw? In transitions like these, fantasy can gain the upper hand over reality, as after months of displacement our feet no longer touched the ground. But of illusions we shall speak more in respect to our life in Paris.

Traveling in this dream, we arrived in Naples, where we remained a month. My father remained near us almost all the time. The Israeli authorities put us up in a midlevel hotel. My stepmother, Odette, went back to Paris to obtain the visa that would allow us to enter France. We ambled through the city and made an excursion to Pompeii. There we walked among the ruins of the city destroyed by the eruption of the volcano and went to the top of Vesuvius by cable car. Since we were very young and had much time to spare, we walked around Naples a lot, a picturesque city like no other. The upper city and the lower city are linked by cornices, and from the heights you discovered the panorama of the bay, a breathtaking view indeed. At first light the voices of the fruit and vegetable merchants in the markets pervaded the entire city. In the alleyways, even the tiny Fiats had trouble getting through. Naples is the kingdom of the horn. At this time I hadn't yet come to know Italian cinema, and this was the first time I was seeing these multicolored clotheslines, hanging like Christmas tinsel garlands between the two sides of the street. To the visitors, but even more so to innocent ones that we were, it provided a feeling of gaiety.

My father left for Paris and returned with the visas and documents that we needed to enter France. He also brought a letter with him from the Israeli embassy in Paris and another from the Jewish agency, certifying that he had paid for the total amount of our trip from Warsaw to Naples as well as for the expenses for the month at the hotel. Quite simply, he was repurchasing us and freeing us. According to the initial visa that got us out from Poland, our luggage was already loaded on the boat to Israel, and he got permission to have it unloaded. This was no small matter, since we were immigrating with the possessions we hadn't sold. We still owned nearly a dozen pieces of luggage, some of them filled with the goose-down comforters and pillows that immigrants from Eastern countries are reluctant to part with and that today still encumber our home closets, even in these days of warming climate. I strongly advise against ever loading all one's trunks on a boat and then having remorse once they are aboard. Unloading luggage from a train is a relatively simple maneuver; getting them off a ship, "good-bye, fare thee well." We were not traveling like guests on a cruise ship, but taking everything we owned. You have to understand that suitcases, trunks, boxes, and small or huge parcels are thrown together into nets, all mixed up, loaded and unloaded by crane. The boat was full of immigrants, and we weren't the only ones traveling with an enormous amount of baggage. The day was entirely taken up with unloading and reloading the deck of the boat in order to look for our belongings in each net. After a few suitcases the captain, an Italian, started to protest and say our bags would be sent back from Haifa. In reality, it was only a strategy to have his palm greased. We had thought this was a system that was the privilege of Russians, but he proved us wrong. When my father slipped him a wad of dollars, he became much more conciliatory. Each net was examined until each piece of luggage was finally recovered.

The Dream of France

My father had to return to Paris, and we left shortly thereafter, still in a slightly unreal state of exhilaration. Nevertheless, we were no longer afraid of anyone. But in spite of everything, our morale wasn't terribly sunny. We arrived in Paris on April 13, 1957. Our journey had taken three and a half months. We weren't superstitious, but the thirteenth did not overly delight us. What was really happening to us was a process of questioning, whether we had made the wrong choice by taking the road to freedom. It certainly can't be said that we were held in a state of captivity in the Soviet Union but rather were in a state of surveilled freedom, a state in which freedom above all was threatened.

When the train pulled in at the Gare de Lyon, a lot of people were there, waiting for us on the platform: my father, his wife, and my nine-year-old sister, as well as an associate of my father and his brother who worked in the company warehouse, with their family. At my father's side were three cousins, two men and one woman I didn't know, and their families. The children of my father's sister were *farbrente komunistn*, fervent Communists in France, and had come to meet me out of curiosity. How could a Communist possibly wish to leave the one and only paradise on earth? There were also acquaintances, some non-Jewish friends of my father and his wife, a dentist with his adult son, as well as several business clients. I had no idea what courteousness or curiosity brought them out to see us. The crowd looked at us like we were from another planet and made gracious gestures and smiles—only a minority spoke Yiddish—to which, considering our communication difficulties, we responded in the friendliest possible way. We could answer only those who spoke Yiddish or Russian to us. The immediate family huddled to figure out how we were all going to fit in the cars, as if it were a wedding. They finally came to an agreement, and we left in the designated cars. I had been placed in a car at the head of the motorcade with my little sister, Françoise. The car was a magnificent Bentley driven by my father's associate. My little sister, Françoise, and I sat in the back seat, but we had a big problem: we had no language in common. So we held each other's hands and got along fine. It was a good omen.

The caravan took the direction of Montfermeil, not far from Paris, where my father owned a property, a big two-story house with a beautiful garden covered in flowers and planted with fruit trees. Just beside it was a small adjoining annex, the lodgings of the couple who looked after the garden and took care of the house. The property was surrounded by an elegant fence with an iron gate. In the house were a majordomo and a cook named Victor. But—I'm still not quite sure—it could have been one and the same person, dressed in a chef's hat and apron in the kitchen, wearing a suit when manning his post in the dining room. Madeleine, who remained many years in the service of Odette and my father, was mainly in charge of taking care of my sister in those days. They also had a maid, and last but not least—Isabelle would keep a souvenir from them—two big Dobermans, mother and daughter, one black and the other chocolate, who were the real guardians of the house.

At first, coming straight from the USSR, the sight of such a lifestyle could have made a positive impression on us. But everyday reality turned out to be a lot different. I was no longer a boy of ten years old. I was a thirty-five-year-old married man and father of two who didn't speak a word of French. One day turned into another, and time was dripping away. We began to have doubts about the reasons for being here. Rose and I undertook to learn French at the Alliance Française. I attended for six months, and she left after three. She had already acquired a solid foundation in high school and was a champion grammarian in any language, getting the best out of the

Alliance. But in such a short time, you can't learn much, other than general principles of the language.

Between me and my father, whom I had not seen for so long, a trench was opening up, perhaps even an abyss. We could never manage to talk about essential things or have even one single sincere conversation where we opened our hearts to each other or found the courage to bare our souls. I never succeeded in telling him what weighed on me and in lancing the boil. Maybe it was my fault. I don't know . . . Unfortunately, that's how it was, and for this sadness we found no remedy. During our trip, as well as in Naples, I related what had been done to my brothers and my mother, how they had been slaughtered like animals by the Germans and Lithuanians. Until the day he died, my father was never able to express anything on the subject. To evoke the loss of his sons, to utter a word in memory of his long-lost wife, to show empathy for their suffering—it was all beyond his strength. For my part, I no longer tried to bring up the subject and behaved as though it didn't exist. His attitude wounded me terribly and to this day causes me enormous sorrow. I felt uncomfortable with him to the point where I asked myself if he had doubts about whether I was his son.

At Montfermeil it was becoming obvious that the two families could no longer live under the same roof. This was not for financial reasons or because there wasn't room enough, but because we were becoming too much for them to bear. We were simply not cut from the same cloth: our manners weren't good enough, we understood nothing of bourgeois codes, and French culture was still inscrutable to us. Our culture was typical of the East, of course by its linguistic components, but also owing to our very popular and working-class character, with its sense of spontaneous irony toward the insignificant nothings that made the recently civilized nouveaux riches appear straitlaced through this lens. After all, my children were very well schooled; my son spoke three languages and read music. We could bring them to fine restaurants without fear that they would eat with their fingers. Anyway, eating with your fingers can be quite agreeable, and the essential principles of life and high culture involve more than just playacting at having manners.

My father and his wife lived lavishly. But our own social and cultural habits put us in positions that could be more than embarrassing. Our sensibilities were always being hurt by situations that seemed to come out of a drama in which we had been cast in secondary roles. Or, rather, it was like we were in a photo novella where the captions below our pictures had been deleted. It was a story without words. Besides not having much talent as an interpreter, my father always seemed to be too far away to help. Conversations followed a lively course, with us as observers. And since we never interrupted and were not ready to participate in the conversation, maybe they thought we had nothing to say. The reality was that we differed in how we saw the world and in our perception of things.

They liked having parties and often had people over. Since we took up four places at the table, they had to limit the number of people they invited. Most of their guests were not Jewish and so did not speak Yiddish. Odette had a lot of friends who were government functionaries or artists. The only one among us who felt at ease and whom everyone wanted to play with was four-year-old Isabelle. She was a Russian-speaking doll. Served at the end of each meal, salad was presented under a different form than in Russia, where it is always cut very small. The first time it was served, Isabelle screamed out in Russian "Ya trava nye kushayu!" (I don't eat grass!), which meant, "Do not take me for a fool . . . or for a cow!"

Let us finally be serious. We had started looking for a way out of our situation. Odette and my father made a decision to sell their property and buy an apartment in Paris, in a chic district, it goes without saying, and, subsequently, to rent another place just for us. In Yiddish we say *mit eyn shos, tsvey hozn,*[1] kill two birds with one stone. They purchased a luxury apartment in an old building near the Eiffel Tower, an entirely residential stretch on the Champ

---

1. Literally: "with one stone, two hares."

de Mars. Some of their workers were let go, but they kept the cook and the housekeeper. During meals, Odette always kept a little hand bell to call the kitchen at the other side of the house, sometimes just to report that a glass was not washed very well. She was always very strict that way.

My father rented a house for us where we still live today and where his sister had lived for forty years. Without any trace of doubt, I can tell you that we felt much better when we moved into our own little place. We could sit around where we wanted to and sleep when we were tired. It was now time to think about our future. We could no longer survive on air and love. To work, we needed papers we still didn't have and to acquire a language we still hadn't mastered. I could no longer remain inactive and began to tap Jewish bosses who spoke Yiddish, for work as a designer of women's clothing. At the time, all the clothing manufacturers were still East European Jews who spoke Yiddish. Today there is not even one left. So I found work easily enough, off the books, naturally. At the beginning, they would have me prepare one design on paper and one on cloth, and once it had been approved by the boss, I would cut all the size gradations in cardboard as a preparatory pattern design for cutting a series. I made these cardboard patterns during the night, at home. At this point of my narrative, it is not a secret that I was accustomed to working nights and not lazy. Nights are long, as everyone knows, and so my children never lacked for anything. In France, as in any other country, the bosses profited from the situation of the immigrants, who could neither read nor write, to pay them *kopkes* and *groshn*,[2] miserable salaries, sometimes as little as a quarter of a normal wage. But it didn't bother me all that much, and I wasn't there to unionize the workers.

Convinced that a man cannot live or be sustained on illusions, that I had to urgently get my feet back on the ground and should count on no one other than myself, I started to react. You could

---

2. *Kopkes* (sing. *kopeck*): the smallest monetary unit of Russia and Belarus; *grosh(n)* is the Yiddish word for a coin.

respond that, compared to other immigrants, I was a privileged one. I was well aware of this myself. Most Jewish immigrants to France who had arrived in 1945 came directly from the camps. For them, life had been without mercy. Compared to the sufferings they had endured, their lot in France must have seemed like a paradise, because, unlike me, they had come without hopes or dreams. The simple fact of being able to rebuild a life was already a miracle. My situation in the Soviet Union had been better than that of so many others. We reunited with my father, not to become rich, but simply for our happiness as a family. The idea of becoming rich was so foreign to us that thinking in those terms could never even enter our minds. More than anything, we missed friendship and love, and we needed being embraced by people. I had felt the bitterness and anger toward my father during childhood and adolescence. During the war there had been no time to dwell on those feelings. To know that my mother and brothers had been exterminated brought terrible sorrow, but no survivor in the postwar period could afford the luxury of expressing it. You had to move forward. Later, when I found out my father was still alive, my heart, so hardened by the war, was softened, as though I had received an electric shock. In Yiddish we would say that blood of the same flesh does not flow like water. I had gone through a relentless war and for years had to stifle my emotions. But feelings had been reawakened when I found out there was another survivor besides me in the family, and even more so when I learned of the existence of a little sister. Tormenting us most was our longing for human and familial warmth. And to this anguish we found no resolution in Paris.

My father was the president, majority owner, and real boss of an important company that made work uniforms. But he had an associate in his employ who had been with him since he was young, had proved himself very capable, and displayed leadership qualities. He was three years older than I was. Before my arrival, he had been allocated shares in the company by way of thanks and had been made a partner, responsible for administrative and commercial issues. The company had government clients, from Air France to the large national utility and transportation services like EDF and SNCF.[3] In order to get large contracts, they had to host high-level administrative types and personally negotiate the contracts. A percentage of the guests at Montfermeil belonged to this caste. My father's young partner was treated like a son . . . When I arrived, he was the one to feel threatened in his plans and ambitions, although I never expressed a single demand or tried to intimidate him in any way. His attitude was owed solely to my mere presence, not my actions. Formally keeping up appearances, he was exceptionally nice to me and always ran eagerly to help me. As my wife's mother used to say, "Vos tsu fil gut teyg nit . . . un vos tsu shlekht teyg gevis nit" (Whatever is overly good is wrong . . . not to speak of what is overly bad). This righteous woman who never complained about her hardship and would have given her last morsel of bread was right. It applied pretty well to the partner's behavior toward me. He had always dreamed of inheriting the business when my father got older. I did nothing either to worry him or to reassure him. I wasn't looking to dispel his fears because I didn't feel guilty. I wasn't even working in the business yet. Even had I ambition to work there, I couldn't because I did not speak French yet. But to him, I was the heir, and that was the only thing on his mind. He should have been more afraid of my sister than of me, but she was still a child and did not pose an immediate risk. A second person was thinking I might come to harm her interests and began to display feelings of jealousy, my stepmother. She was afraid she would see my father change toward her and transfer his love to me. Unfortunately, I never felt any such thing—quite the contrary. She worried about the future, imagining that he was going to leave me millions or at least that he was liable to leave me part of his fortune while leaving her penniless. De facto, she was a logical ally of the partner. To me, far from hating her, I liked and respected her a lot.

3. EDF: Electricité de France, the nationally owned electricity company. SNCF: Société nationale des chemins de fer français, France's nationally owned railway company.

Younger than my father, Odette was as naïve as a spoiled child, and that was somehow the basis of her relationship with him. With a lot of intelligence, she showed a kindness toward me, and especially the children. In her childlike attitude, she desired to see them become *de vrais Français*, right and proper people blessed with good manners and good education. Beginning with the external, she had taken Sacha to have a short crew cut, à la Poujade,[4] which was apparently the bourgeois style in those days. Very attached to the children, she often took Sacha home with her and took care of him, especially later on when I had to work in the North of France. She got up very early to take him to the Maimonides school in Boulogne where he was enrolled. She also took him horseback riding and on weekends went out with the two kids on cultural activities she had planned. Aware of Isabelle's personality, and an art lover herself, she would take her to museums and antique markets when she was barely eight years old. According to my daughter she played a major role in opening her mind to art and culture. She also took her regularly to the steam baths in the rue de Rosiers, where Odette used to meet her circle and where Isabelle became the mascot of this little social scene. My father also loved the children and spoiled them. He loved to come over for lunch, lie down for a little nap, and then take Sacha for a walk in the city. On one afternoon's excursion with his grandson he complained of pain in his feet, though he was a good walker. Upon closer examination, it was revealed that he had put on two left shoes.

Coming from the USSR, where all Jewish culture had been repressed, Rose absolutely insisted that the children go to Jewish schools and grow up with a Jewish education and within a Jewish culture. In retrospect, I think she was absolutely right because they both received from this teaching, at the Lucien de Hirsch school where they were taught Hebrew and later, for Sacha, at the Maimonides high school, a knowledge we undoubtedly never could have transmitted

4. In the style of Pierre Poujade, a right-wing populist politician after whom the Poujadist movement was named.

to them. Unfortunately, these private and expensive schools were still not within our means, and my father took the responsibility for paying the first year. The children learned French very quickly, which had helped us in return to improve our skills from them. When I began speaking a little, my father and his partner offered me a job as director of a factory located between Lille and Lens, two hundred kilometers from Paris. It was paradoxical, illogical, and even incredible when you considered how little assimilated I still was.

This factory in the little village of Provin, of no more than a thousand inhabitants, in the North of France, made work clothes. Most of the orders came from the state or from semiprivate firms and were intended for the train and electricity companies' workers, coal miners, civil aviation employees, and also shopkeepers. Part of the merchandise was for retail stores, and the rest supplied markets and fairs. We employed more than two hundred people, mostly women. There were about twenty cutters, mostly men. They cut more than three thousand meters of material every day, and the assembly line turned out around two thousand items per day. The factory truck made deliveries to Paris twice a week. It was into this whirlpool that they wanted to parachute me. I was offered the work . . . but no one forced me to accept it, and when I finally did, I didn't know if they wished me well or ill . . . At the time, I did not think I was ready; it was much too soon.[5] I admit to having been in a state of real panic in the face of this challenge. When I first visited the factory, I was introduced not as the director but as the boss's son. Relationships in this part of France were still very paternalistic, if not medieval. The workers, who made up more or less the entire working-age population of the village, spoke a patois that had not the slightest resemblance to the French I was learning in Paris. They conducted themselves toward me with a deference and fear that I had never seen before in any of my work relationships. Being treated like a king with

5. While reading his manuscript, Moishe uttered out loud, three times, *dray pintelekh* (ellipses) in the last few sentences, insisting on the irony of his situation.

no crown was embarrassing. The workers had little education and were trained on the job for a single position. The girls, hired much too young, had a problem with self-control that was quite striking. They had not yet acquired the constitution needed to follow the pace of assembly-line work. Occasionally, after a nervous crisis, they left the line in tears, and a replacement would then have to be found.

I too was frustrated, but not for the same reason. I missed my comrades and friends and was filled with nostalgia. I had lost all my wartime comrades with whom I had been linked by friendship and blood. I was burdened with painful feelings. The work did not frighten me, and I had no doubts as to my abilities to oversee it. I was used to being a leader. Very young I had led soldiers and been responsible for their lives. After the war I was for three years at the head of the vocational school where there were a lot more people than at the Provin factory. I had been a union secretary in the party. What was making me so uncomfortable and causing me such anxiety was my lame French. I was lacking a great deal of vocabulary, which was also true for my writing. I had to dictate to my secretary, who typed what I said, and the words I didn't know couldn't be told in Yiddish, since I was the one and only Jew in town. In a word, my French was bad. In spite of everything, I very quickly began to learn patois.

When I arrived, the departing director was still there and did not welcome me with open arms. He had already received his letter of dismissal for serious mistakes. Upon meeting him, I understood the urgency of being parachuted in. He had to hand over all the accounts to me, and it didn't take long before I understood how things were supposed to be run. I even had the advantage of being experienced in the profession. When I began running things, I reorganized certain of the assembly lines that then started producing more pieces than before, then focused on the cutting practices in place, and ended up devising ways to save on material. When thousands of meters of material are cut, a few centimeters saved from each piece amounts to a lot of money in the end. The timing of the work stations is also very important in lowering costs. I had been very well trained in rationalizing work and obtaining maximum yields to fill a quota.

Such exploitation of workers might have seemed intolerable to a former Marxist. But the truth is that Soviet-style socialism, which was socialism in name only, did not teach pity for the workers for the good reason, using their logic, that the workers themselves were "in power." There was, so to speak, nothing else but the working class, and therefore what we called the "dictatorship of the proletariat." And a dictatorship it was. Words like *pity* or *ethics* were nonexistent. What's more, since I didn't know the real reason they had sent me this far from Paris, whether I was in hell or purgatory, I could not allow myself to make mistakes or produce at the same costs. I was in the grip of my own contradictions.

I would spend the working week in Provin, where I was the only resident who wasn't from the village. On weekends, I returned home to Paris. I had at my disposal a small commercial Citroën with a van body in the rear, a *Deux-Chevaux*, so loaded down with special orders that I could not see out the back. When I got to Paris, I dropped off the orders at the company. We also used the little van for the weekends, loading the kids into the back like little piglets. How much would you guess this kind of car consumes in gasoline? I can tell you: nothing but three liters, so now just imagine . . . One fine day—as a matter of fact, I don't remember what this day looked like—my father's partner calls me into his office and says, "You know, Moishe," or in fact, Maurice, as they had begun calling me, "it seems to me you're using too much gas. I was looking at your gas receipts. It's really too much." I was thinking to myself, what chutzpah, the nerve he had, to raise such a ridiculous issue. What were his ulterior motives? Obviously, it wasn't a question of a few liters of gas. The real reason for these ludicrous remarks was that he couldn't stand the fact that the factory in Provin was producing more than ever before. I screwed up my courage and answered back: "And you, I don't see you taking long walks, either. You've got a big English thirty-horsepower car registered to the business that does not take three liters but fifteen to go the same distance. Is someone criticizing you over it? Not even me!" He turned as white as a sheet and began trying to justify himself and persuade me that he didn't mean to hurt me. That was the end of the story, right then and there. He never tried anything like that again.

I never mentioned the incident to my father. On the other hand, a little later, my father gave me a gift of a brand-new sky-blue Aronde that even got us to Portugal via Spain. But the minute I had a little money, I sold it and bought on credit a used Déesse, the "goddess," Citroën's luxury model at the time, which also went into service for the company. I wanted, naturally, to show my father's partner that I was not his subordinate but was at the end of the day my father's son. We spoke only about work, and he made a visible effort to stay in his lane and not hurt me again.

Time went by quickly, and I had already been at the factory for two years. For me it wasn't a normal life, and for my family even less so. Rose wanted us to rent a house and for us to live together. So we moved into a villa a little too large for us, surrounded by a garden, not far from the factory. We bought some beds, and Rose, Isabelle, and I moved into an almost empty house. Isabelle was enrolled in the primary school, where she made friends quickly. She loved the countryside. Sacha stayed in Paris at the Maimonides boarding school and periodically went back to stay with Odette and my father. Our village was small and had nothing to offer in the way of things to do. There was only one small café. Rose decided to get her driving permit at Lens and began driving the Déesse. She took it to go shopping at the market in Carvin, a few kilometers away.

But it was no use—this particular exile wasn't for me. If they wanted it, I would trade the high-level job right back to them, but I just didn't want any more of living out in the country. I let my father know I wanted to come back to Paris. Three years had been enough, I told him. He reminded me that on my own initiative, I had created another workshop in a nearby village that manufactured dress pants. I had even hired a designer to draw patterns. "Who's going to look after the workshop and run it, and what are you going to do in Paris?" asked my father. He and his partner had already planned to expand production by building a large modern one-story factory, with a capacity for two thousand pieces a day. It was located in Lorient, which was offering easy terms for construction in order to create jobs in their industrial zone. This factory was built a few years later. At this very moment, I decided that they were going to have to do it without me. The only thing I had on my mind was getting myself out of the countryside and even out of the firm.

The back-and-forth went on. While waiting for something else to come along, I offered to cut, in Paris, the pants that were being cut in Lorient and send them back to the factory for assembly. I returned to Paris, and they hired another director, a Sephardic Jew who arrived from North Africa in these years. As a matter of fact, I had a totally different plan in mind. I had resolved to leave my father's company, as we say in Yiddish, *makhn mayn shabbes far zikh aleyn*, to set my own *shabbes*, so that no one could ever again have the opportunity to be jealous of me. For better or worse, I was to become a business-man without a partner. About commerce, I knew absolutely nothing. How do you eat this dish? But . . . if you could teach horses to dance.

My father helped me with a modest sum, key money for a small space. It wasn't much, but for me it was fine. I had come from a society where everything belonged to the state, where should you want to buy anything, you were standing in interminable lines in front of stores empty of goods. In France the customer is king and one waits on the client. You have to adapt to the laws of supply and demand. The customer buys only what suits him, and even then you have to add a little dose of persuasion and not forget for a moment that the customer is always right. It was all Greek to me, and until I understood how things worked, we suffered a lot. At the back of the shop was a tiny workshop where I hand-produced various designs for the haute couture, especially reversible clothes. If we didn't complete them at the shop, I finished the work at home with Rose. As usual, and as it had always been in my life of a laborer, the nights were long. We worked in this store until retirement. We did not get rich because we never had the necessary ambition, but we ended up learning our trade and were ultimately able to avoid contract work. We earned a reasonable living and saved for a decent retirement, paying a lot of dues and contributing to pension funds.

We were satisfied with our lives, raising our children and seeing them get married. They gave us grandchildren who are very dear to us and that we love tenderly and who give back in kind. As for our children, we can sense how close they are to us. They give us a lot of love, perhaps more than what we have been able to give them. If I tell you in Yiddish that we would say "they carry us in their arms," which means they cherish us, it might seem exaggerated, but that is exactly our feeling. A child's love can be neither measured nor expressed, only felt. In our family, everyone was attached to the other, and we didn't know what it meant to argue or quarrel, and not for lack of discussion. We knew nothing of that worst thing, what began with two brothers in Genesis, between Cain and Abel: jealousy, which is still, sadly, all too common. What we have always wished for most in the world is for peace to reign in the family as it should reign between people and beliefs. As for my little sister, Françoise, we are very close and just as close with her husband, a good and exceptional man. My niece, Cécile, their daughter, is also very attached to our family, and we consider her one of our own children.

So now I've told you the story of my life, of our lives together, without going into minute detail but without omitting the most important things. What a relief to finish this manuscript! To get back to the most important point, I must one last time evoke my lost family, may they rest in peace. Sixty years have passed, and it has become difficult to remember their faces; they appear as through a veil of sleep or a dream. Even when I look at their pictures, their faces are still not restored to my memory. I do not remember what my brothers looked like. As for my mother, it is not any easier. A time machine would be the only thing to help. But I make an effort to make them come alive and to represent them as they might be today, or even a mere twenty years ago. My mother, may she rest in peace, was a marvelous human being and highly sensitive, and she possessed an exceptional courteousness and thoughtfulness. Her health was fragile. Because of her heart condition, she spent most of her time seated in a chair, a book in her hands. When I was six or seven, I did something wrong, nothing unusual for me, just one of my classic tricks, so I managed to hide on the roof of our two-floor house to escape my father's anger. My mother came outside to reassure me and get me off my perch: "Meyshele, come and eat. Your father has already forgiven you." I came down and got away with a mild punishment for my misdeeds. My mother always advocated with a soothing word, never having to raise her voice.

As for my brothers, may they rest in peace, my older brother, Yosef, did not talk a lot. He spent most of his time outside of the house, and he resembled my mother through his calm demeanor. My younger brother Leybe was even calmer than my mother, and the youngest, Elie, was a beautiful boy with light brown, almost golden, curls and blue eyes. He was a pleasant and affectionate child who sought affection from those around him, perhaps because he had never known his father. He was two when I left home to work and ten years old when I saw him for the last time. In spite of every sort of problem my mother had to face, she succeeded in maintaining a high moral standard in a house full of boys, and while I was sent off to work, my brothers all continued to study. Arguments were very rare, almost nonexistent, and self-discipline was a rule in the household, naturally emanating from the respect we had for all the decisions my mother made regarding important issues. She had a sense of fairness none of us would ever have thought to question, squaring the domestic shortages and distributing whatever the household had, the fat and the lean in equal measure.

With the passing of years, I think I have inherited from her a certain serenity that has allowed me to master a nature that was pretty fiery to begin with. In her quiet manner, eschewing pompous speech as well as gesticulations, my mother imprinted on me an ethic that I was reminded of every time I strayed from it. To her I owe having always been upright to my friends, to my family, and to Rose's.

Leafing through the Pages
with an Open Heart

> My grandfather used to say: "Life is astonishingly short.
> Thinking back now, I can hardly understand how, for instance,
> a young man could even decide to ride his horse to the next
> village putting aside any worries about the fact that—barring
> any possible accidents—the timespan of an ordinary, happily
> flowing life would never suffice for such a ride."
> —Franz Kafka, *Das nächste Dorf*
> (1919), translated by Yeva Lapsker

Before I end my autobiography I'd like to take a few pages to deal
with my state of mind at the time I stopped working and went into
retirement. A man does not live only to satisfy his physical and material needs. As I understand and feel it, a man must also nourish his
mind and his soul. The reality is that half the world is so disinherited
that it is reduced to problems of immediate survival. In spite of such
terrible conditions, men have a stubborn persistence toward spirituality. The spirit needs every substance that can nourish hope, for who
can live without hope? And should the advantages of a normal life
be his, he has a tendency to feed his hope with delusions and errors,
be they ideologies, religious beliefs, or the dogmas that are à la mode
at the moment. Some may find, or believe they find, a spiritual path
by joining cults that manipulate and indoctrinate them for often dis-
reputable ends.

Having gone through several stages of life, I feel the need to explain
how I evolved from a childhood in a traditional family—though

broken by the departure of my father—where my mother and grand-parents were very pious, as I was supposed to be, to become a practic-ing Marxist. How is it that now, as a mature man, I am returning to a religious and spiritualist approach to the world? In this biographi-cal narrative I have recounted the journey of a ten-year-old proletar-ian, to young union organizer, and finally a Communist in the army. Anyone who has been a Marxist, and what's more a hardened Com-munist, indoctrinated to the highest degree through systematic train-ing, does not become a believer in God and an observant Jew from one day to the next. In my case, it was on the contrary the object of a years-long reflection and a long process. At first, I ignored where these meditations would lead me or that it would be necessary to submit the greater part of my life to analysis, from my earliest years to age sixty-five. There came a moment, however, where the need to draw a line in respect of my past and face up to the future became imperative.

Without any affectedness or exaggeration, my wife had always stayed firmly attached to her beliefs and to the religion of her parents, while I was the opposite. In those things she thought of as essential, I gave in to her demands, even if it they rubbed up against my Marx-ist ideology. Over the years, I cannot say she had no influence on my thinking. As I wrote earlier, I fasted for the first time since my youth on Yom Kippur on the eve of leaving the Soviet Union. Arriving in Paris, I reserved seats at the synagogue attached to the school my children attended where I would go on the High Holidays, abstaining from going to work. But truth be told, I did all of it to please my wife and to give my kids an education, and certainly not because I cared then deeply about spirituality. When the time came to retire, my head was empty, my heart was empty, and I was also very nervous, so I scrambled for a remedy for my growing feeling of discontent. Not knowing how to occupy my free time, I began reading a lot and lis-tening to classical music, which soothed me. I had always loved to read. I reread the great Russian classics in French and began devour-ing French novels and history books. I read the complete works of Shakespeare and reread them without missing a beat. *The Merchant of Venice* had always fascinated and intrigued me by its stereotypical caricature of the Jew. The frescoes of Alexandre Dumas brought me closer and more familiar to French history.

I also turned toward Jewish history, beginning with Flavius Josephus, followed by contemporary histories of Judaism, and finally I understood that if I really wanted to understand something about Jewish history, I couldn't avoid reading the Bible. It was a period when I was reading more than I could absorb. It was not to accumulate knowledge, but because I was like a child who was wandering in overgrown shrubs and looking for a way out.

Apparently, I could not survive without either ideology or religion, simply with my nose in a daily routine. So I then decided to read philosophy, and not the philosophy that had been professed at the Marxist university, but rather all the ancient and modern authors of every school of thought. I have here to confess that I love philosophy, but that I am not particularly fond of philosophers. Of course, they are men of high caliber who must demonstrate their wisdom, rely on their knowledge of the world, and think methodically. But every one of them seems to possess the absolute truth, even though they swear that they are searching only for a truth that is relative.

From where I stand, no assertion of truth can have absolute value. It isn't my intention to give lessons to the philosophers; I am not learned enough for that. I am a simple man and do not pretend in any case to be holding the truth. But this does not take away my right to think and to an ordinary man's opinion. Philosophers refer to metaphysics to demonstrate the existence of God. The term was first used by Aristotle. But Spinoza interested me more, because he was a Jew and because he dealt at length with the existence of God. I first had to read his books several times before I began to understand what he meant. His very conceptual writing is complex and can even seem quite muddled when he resorts to geometric or axiomatic methods borrowed from mathematics to establish a metaphysical argument and to demonstrate the existence of God. His books were written for the cream among philosophers, for the intellectuals of his time. From the outset, I was attracted to his political and

economic philosophy, by his theories of democracy and the separation of church and state. Offspring of a Marrano family that had
moved to Amsterdam, Baruch de Spinoza was born in 1632 and died
in 1677. His father was a member of the Mahamad, the assembly
of Portuguese Jews in Amsterdam. Spinoza started out as a pious
Jew, a descendant of crypto-Jews who were themselves the progeny
of those so-called New Christians. The Marranos are the Jews who
continued practicing a form of their faith in secrecy after their expul-
sion from Spain and Portugal.[1] Amsterdam had become a fairly lib-
eral place of refuge where the Marranos, returning openly to their
ancestral faith, ended up becoming strict interpreters of the oral and
written law, perhaps through a misreading of the Torah, which they
were only just rediscovering.

I would like to pause and discuss the way Spinoza broached the
problem of theology. This is not a sudden venture into theological
polemics, but truly because it collides with my own approach to faith,
as with my way of grasping the Old Testament. I will not touch on
questions of democracy, civil liberty, ethics, or politics, which Spinoza
tackled in his works on the state. What I wish to speak of is the scrip-
tural freedom that he claims for all times and all places. Let's look
concretely at a summary of what I have been able to extrapolate after
a thorough reading. His definition of God: "1) God is a supremely
perfect being; 2) God is an absolutely infinite being; 3) God is a being
whose essence pertains to existence; 4) God is a being that is defined
by having infinite attributes."[2] For Spinoza, God can be described as

1. As it is obvious from the previous pages about Moishe's extending readings
over the years, books have circulated between Moishe Rozenbaumas's home and
his daughter's. For sure he had read the *History of Marranos* by Cecil Roth, as well
as everything available in the four volumes of *La société juive à travers l'histoire*,
under the direction of Shmuel Trigano.

2. Benedict de Spinoza, *Ethics*, vol. 2 of *Chief Works*, trans. Robert Harvey
Monro Elwes: "By God, I mean a being absolutely infinite—that is, a substance
consisting in infinite attributes, of which each expresses eternal and infinite essen-
tiality" (45). I am grateful to Amélie Ducroux, who helped me locate the quotes

constructed from his attributes. However, he distinguishes the world described by speech, which is an attribute of man, from the attributes of an extended world and a thinking world, the attributes of God. He adds that reason is light—understood as an emanation of nature— of thought. Without this light, thought can apprehend nothing but dreams and fictions. And it is this last detail on the nature of God that renders the first four problematic, even if at first glance we would be attempting to accept it like the others. Even if we were to accept the four primary definitions of God, how could man possess attributes, even a single attribute, not belonging to God.

He writes, "Knowing this, I next asked [in chapter 3] why the Hebrews were called God's chosen people? When I saw that this was only because God had chosen a certain land for them, where they could live securely and [III/10] comfortably, from that I learned that the laws God revealed to Moses were nothing but the legislation of the particular state of the Hebrews, and that no one else was obliged to accept them, indeed that even the Hebrews were bound by them only so long as their state lasted."[3] If Spinoza is admitting that God gave his laws to Moses, these laws could not have been given with an expiration date, the time the Hebrew state would last. If the law is of divine origin and received as such by those who in the time of Moses were called Hebrews and then Israelites, and finally Jews, it can have been given only for all times and all places. Further on, he writes: "Every one must be left free to think what he wants and to say what he thinks. The God who speaks to men's imaginations through Moses and the prophets, in Scripture, can provide no teaching on the question of the relationship between revelation and the truth gleaned from natural light. A few doubts must be entertained

---

in the English editions of the authors Moishe Rozenbaumas is discussing in this chapter.

3. Edition used by Moishe Rozenbaumas: Baruch de Spinoza, *Oeuvres II: Traité théologico-politique*, trans. Charles Appuhn (Paris: Garnier-Flammarion, 1965); *The Collected Works of Spinoza*, ed. and trans. Edwin Curley (Princeton, NJ: Princeton Univ. Press, 2016), e71.

about attributing to Moses every part of the Pentateuch, or to Joshua the book in his name." He then goes on to explain that the transcriptions of the five books was done with slavish fidelity and without any criticism by Israelite scribes, produced in a limited number of copies, perhaps two or three. According to Spinoza, the superstitious respect professed for a literal version prevented a critical spirit from being applied to the canon. He doesn't deal with freedom in one place alone but in all places and for all times. In his *Tractatus Theologico-Politicus*, he affirms that the God of the Jews and Christians is another name for the "totality of the strictly fundamental natural powers." The human being, a prey to fears entrenched in his imagination, conjures the gods. His conclusion is that "we are not forced to have to hold on to our faith in the prophets." If, as Spinoza thinks, Moses could not have spoken face-to-face with God because no one can look on the face of God and that no image of God appeared to Moses, then no law was revealed to the Israelites, neither for that time nor for any other.

In his lifetime, Spinoza's work aroused reactions of horror and revulsion in Amsterdam's Spanish-Portuguese Jewish community that led to his excommunication, the redoubtable *herem*, the ban that excludes an individual from his community. He died alone and in poverty in 1677. When all his household goods were sold, there was still not enough to pay for his burial. He was dead, but Spinozism remained alive, opposed by numerous detractors over the centuries yet also admired among philosophers and intellectuals. When his work was published posthumously, Spinozism garnered also the hatred of Calvinist rigorists. The young Marx, while he was a student, could hardly be ignorant of Heinrich Heine's words that all contemporary philosophers were unaware of looking at the world through lenses polished by Spinoza. Marx summed up his disagreement with Spinoza saying, "Ignorance is not an argument." He considered Spinoza a "sick animal" and rejected his political, economic, and especially his social ideas.

Spinoza's derogatory ideas about the books attributed to Moses and to the prophets poisoned his relationship with Amsterdam's

Jewish community. But in his theological writings, he had yet dedicated considerable effort and many pages to demonstrate the existence of God. When a man believes in God, he feels it; he fears him;
he certainly doesn't feel the need to prove his/her/its existence by
means of geometric formulas and is attached to his belief through
all the fibers of his body. He covets the idea that the human being
was created by God in his/her/its image, that life and death belong to
God, and that all of man's actions and the world's as well are divinely
derived. Spinoza contested the very bedrock assumptions of the Bible
and the commandments and rejected the prophets, especially Moses.
In the eyes of the Jewish community of his time, that was his most
serious sin; he was tampering with the foundations of the Jewish
house, which was at risk of collapse. Jewish believers had passed on
the law and the commandments from generation to generation. If
Jews had faith and were not posing the question of God's existence,
then who was he writing for? My sense is that he was writing to
arouse the curiosity of philosophers and intellectuals. Spinoza called
for the right to speak and think in complete freedom, everywhere
and with no strings attached. No matter how great the attempt, a
human being cannot be prevented from thinking; no one can control
someone else's thought, even less his or her subconscious. The brain
of an individual belongs to this person alone, and even under the
worst dictatorship, no one can have access to the intimate thoughts
of another. But freedom to speak and to write was going to lead to
disorder and confusion, one way or the other. When a congregant
interrupts and contradicts a rabbi in the middle of a discourse in a
house of prayer, he is inevitably creating a condition of dissent. Was
this the freedom of speech on which Spinoza insisted? In his Amsterdam community, that was exactly what he did, when preaching freedom of speech about the Bible. I don't know if there was such a place
where questions could be brought up in the same way they are today
when everyone can take the floor to express a view. The fact remains
that dissension broke out.

What God did Spinoza believe in that he had so much need to
prove its existence? For me, it's difficult to grasp. I tend to think that

he no longer believed in anything and was offering up an intellectual demonstration that deprecated the Amsterdam community and Jewish belief, while also taking revenge at his excommunication. Which Jewish believer, or even anyone faithful to his origins, could accept his approach or his conclusions? The Jewish people have survived thanks only to the Book and the Oral Law.[4] In draining them of their content, Spinoza even undermined the foundation of all belief and all affiliation. His writings were addressed to atheists and to the great intellectuals of his time. He aimed at becoming their peer. Even if his writing is marked more by Judaism than he liked to admit, he always referred to Judaism in the third person, as though he never had himself been a Jew or a member of the community.

Spinoza admitted to the possibility of human error: "I know that I am a man and may have erred. Still, I have taken great care not to err, and taken care especially that whatever I might write would be entirely consistent with the laws of my country, with piety and with morals."[5] In all of his writings, Spinoza showed himself to be very prudent to not cross the Dutch authorities and exercised his freedom to criticize vis-à-vis the church with much caution. These precautions were not as critical when it came to the Jewish community. Today, his comments and his writings would obviously not lead to a *herem* pronounced against him, theological questions being widely debated in the community, both from the religious perspective as well as from all currents of Jewish thought. The four volumes of Shmuel Trigano[6]

4. According to rabbinic Judaism, the Oral Torah or Oral Law (תורה שבעל פה, *Torah she-be-ʿal peh*, literally "Torah that is on the mouth") represents those laws, statutes, and legal interpretations that were not recorded in the Five Books of Moses, the Written Torah (תורה שבכתב, *Torah she-bi-khtav*, literally "Torah that is in writing").

5. Benedict de Spinoza, "Theological-Political Treatise," in *The Collected Works of Spinoza*, 1:75–76.

6. Shmuel Trigano, *La société juive a travers l'histoire*, 4 vols. (Paris: Fayard, 1992–93), vol. 1, *La fabrique du peuple*; vol. 2, *Les liens de l'alliance*; vol. 3, *Le passage d'Israël*; vol. 4, *Le peuple monde*.

are good demonstrations that there has not always been *sholem-bays*, domestic peace, in Judaism or among its rabbis and that passionate conflicts have always torn the unity of the Jewish religion. With the emergence of the Haskalah, the Jewish Enlightenment, and the rise of Hasidism, the struggle between this new mystical movement and Misnagdim[7] raged for decades and gave rise to reciprocal excommunications. The Shulchan Aruch, the codification of Jewish law, gave rise to arguments lasting decades, before any accord could be reached. But no one went as far as Spinoza in challenging the foundations of Judaism. Jewish religion has survived in spite of so much, and even among nonbelievers the validity of the Ten Commandments is not fundamentally suspected. Whatever philosophers and intellectuals may have to say about it, the Torah existed before they did and will remain intact after them, while Jews will continue to believe in scripture and the Bible or find in them a source of renewal. Yet one must admit that the books Spinoza wrote to discuss ethics and the problem of the state were very much ahead of their time.

To close the reflections inspired by my reading Spinoza and pondering his relationship to the religious question, it seems to be that he erred because his hostility to his community pushed him to elaborate philosophical ideas that did not accord with his own religious conviction. At no point in his work does he declare himself an atheist, but his criticism often evokes a desire for vengeance and ranks him among the atheists. It seems to me that perhaps he went beyond his own philosophy, endowing his work with a clear-cut character, vehement and overly definitive, which weakens the sincerity of philosophical doubt that is indispensable in the search for all truth.

Nietzsche, born in Germany in 1844 and living until 1900, interests me as a non-Jewish thinker expressing himself on the sacred books and the Old Testament. As opposed to Spinoza, his approach to Judaism is imbued with respect, and I find it interesting that he

---

7. Misnagdim מתנגדים; also Mitnagdim is a Hebrew word meaning "opponents." The term refers to opponents of Hasidism.

had the nerve to criticize all philosophers. Perhaps too much . . . I don't know if he can be classified as a philosopher. I think he is recognized by philosophers today in spite of his critiques. His extremist ideas advocate for a new society, with a new man, strong and aristocratic, an unmixed race. This one requirement for an unmixed race is perplexing, if not disturbing. How does it fit in? How can one interpret that? I prefer to think that his system comes closer to an intellectual feat than to a political program. I especially studied his book *Beyond Good and Evil* in which he takes up different questions, such as the critique of the modern mind, without omitting science, modern art, or politics and ethics. Let's take the example of what Nietzsche wrote on the Jews:

> The Jews—a people "born for slavery," as Tacitus and the entire ancient world said, "the chosen people among peoples," as they themselves said and believed—the Jews achieved the amazing feat of inverting values, thanks to which life on earth for two millennia has possessed a new and dangerous appeal. Their prophets fused "rich," "godless," "evil," "violent," and "sensuous" into a unity and for the first time coined the word "world" as a word connoting shame. In this inversion of values (to which belongs the use of the word for "poor" as a synonym for "holy" and "friend") lies the significance of the Jewish people: with them begins the *slave rebellion in morality.*[8]

8. This translation by Ian Johnston of F. Nietzsche, *Beyond Good and Evil* (Arlington, VA: Richer Resources, 2009), is slightly closer to M. Rozenbaumas's translation of his French version into Yiddish. Considered more reliable is also Walter Kaufmann's translation of F. Nietzsche, *Beyond Good and Evil: Prelude to a Philosophy of the Future* (New York: Random House, 1966): "The Jews—a people 'born from slavery,' as Tacitus and the whole ancient world say; 'the chosen people among the peoples,' as they themselves say and believe—the Jews have brought off that miraculous feat of an inversion of values, thanks to which life on earth has acquired a novel and dangerous attraction for a couple of millennia: their prophets have fused 'rich,' 'godless,' 'evil,' 'violent,' and 'sensual' into one and were the first to use the word 'world' as an opprobrium. This inversion of values (which

This avalanche of praise, for our people and our Bible, formulated during Nietzsche's time, is certainly heartwarming. He considered Judaism, and prophetism in particular, to have introduced an overthrow of the values of the ancient world. His writings remain a reference. I accept them. On the other hand, what he wrote of the Übermensch, on castes, on hierarchy, as well as the tableau he paints of an imaginary society led by aristocratic castes appears to me to be the fruit of his fantasies. The audacity with which he rejects democracy, against the course of history, nevertheless demonstrates his capacity to invent a new system and affirms his authority as a thinker.

In his time, the tendency toward assimilation of certain circles of the Jewish population, mostly among the bourgeoisie and intellectuals, went all the way to conversion, not only with the hope of penetrating the Gentile society and avoiding their hatred, but especially to improve their own economic condition and make inroads into professional sectors where Jews didn't have the right to work. Let's take the example of Heinrich Heine (1797–1856), born in Düsseldorf. To his great distress, when he wanted to apply for a professorship, Jews were still excluded from the university. He then decided to convert to Protestantism, bringing upon himself hatred from Jews and even more the hatred of non-Jews. From this experience he developed a profound bitterness that he expressed in his writings:

> My ancestors belonged to the noble house of Israel and I am a great grandson of a martyred people which gave the world the creator of moral philosophy, and fought and suffered on humanity's battlefields of mind and thought. . . . In spite of the *shtreiml* (the traditional fur hat worn by Hasidic Jews) on their head and the barbaric ideas in their heads, I have more appreciation for Polish Jews than for those of Germany because and thanks to their isolation, and because of the character of the Polish Jews that evolved to near

---

includes using the word 'poor' as synonymous with 'holy' and 'friend') constitutes the significance of the Jewish people: they mark the beginning of the slave rebellion in morals" (108).

perfection. Polish Jews, with their grimy fur, their long beard, and the odor of garlic they propagate, with their Yiddish jargon, to me, are more affectionate, closer to my heart than other Jews, swimming in equity valuations and the trends of the stock markets.[9]

Heine always fiercely defended the freedom of the poet, whose best weapon was creative eloquence. Please excuse me for having here translated Heine from the Yiddish jargon that he loved and that I love as well. Maybe it is "poetic justice" that this Jew, who was at the apex of German literature, is being read in Yiddish.

Despite emancipation and assimilation, hatred of Jews continued without pause. And even once they had imagined that conversion would protect them, they were never spared gratuitous hatred.

Finally, I want to say that philosophers, with all the respect I grant them, are not prophets. They are men like other men. They are not immune to error, and there is nothing absolute in their thought that at times even goes astray. Neither the philosophers nor the intellectuals or free thinkers have succeeded in turning Jewish believers away from their faith. We have to recognize the fact that the Torah has been passed down from century to century thanks to the chain of generations who received and then bequeathed an authentic religious education.

I now return to my search to find my own way. It seems that I have arrived at a certain mastery of my being. I ended up by finding God. And it is not a discovery that one makes by looking under a pillow. You must feel that he is here and that he protects not only you but all human beings. Only he who has faith, who believes in the Torah with all his conviction, also fears God. It is not my intention to influence anyone in their belief or their ideology, not even my

9. "Über Polen" [On Poland], *Sämtliche Schriften* (1823), 2:69. The editor was unable to locate this quote in the Yiddish translation of Heinrich Heine, *Di verk fun Haynrikh Hayne miṭ a biografye fun A. Ḳalisher un a forvorṭ fun N. Sirḳin* (New York: Farlag, 1918). Available online at the National Yiddish Book Center: https://archive.org/details/nybc207115/page/n4.

daughter . . . I speak for myself and myself alone and of my relationship to religion. I have already been on the other side of the fence and have served other gods. The person who believes in the Torah must accept it as it is, indivisible. One cannot say, "I'll take this. This pleases me, but that doesn't," or "We must change this and that." It must be taken as a unit and not have anything cut away.

There are those who say that certain things in the Torah have to change, in order to adapt it to the modern world. True enough, the application of its laws is subject to many interpretations. Take, for example, the most burning question to face contemporary Jewish society, all over the world and even in Israel. According to Halacha, Jewish law, a child born of a non-Jewish mother and a Jewish father is not a Jew. To become Jewish in his own right, this person must convert like any other non-Jew. If memory serves, in long-gone times the succession was passed through the father, so there certainly have been changes in the laws. It would sometimes take several centuries for the rabbis to make a decision on a point of Halacha. This sort of question cannot be resolved from the outside in the manner of an ukase, and today it has become a most pressing problem for Jewish society. The rabbinic authorities must not wait centuries to confront this absolute emergency, which touches on the very existence of the Jewish people. Only a competent, higher religious authority, gathering all currents together, would have the necessary authority to make changes.

Along the same lines, I have trouble with the so-called very Orthodox, lacking the indispensable qualities to demonstrate a more humane approach toward their nonpracticing coreligionists, thereby marginalizing nonobservant Jews. Even if it is unintended, a Jew who performs a daily mitzvah is as good as a strictly religious man to me. I do not measure a man's piety by the length of his beard or his *payes* (sidelocks). God listens to everyone, and he who prays sincerely does not need exterior signs or physical demonstrations. It's a subject that we could discuss at length. A person who enters a synagogue today, who has known the piety without affectation of the traditional Jewish world of old, will know what I am talking about.

For me, everything was complicated from the start. I somehow imagined that most of these people, some of them bearded Jews—which was so uncommon in Lithuania, even before the war—earned their living from religious activities. I also thought they were not sociable and very reluctant to connect with new congregants. But when on tiptoe I started to attend synagogue, I found men who were normal and familiar and who took more of an interest in other people than did other population groups. They knew who among them was celebrating a happy occasion and who was in bereavement. I experienced enormous difficulty during these first tentative steps to attend prayer services, as I had forgotten how to read Hebrew and wondered how to start over again. There were people who saw my distress and embarrassment. Some were cordial and helped me and did not look down on my pitiable first steps. At the time, I was not far away from my seventieth birthday, and I was struggling to reach the level of a boy of ten. When I saw the education and the knowledge they were giving to their children, all that was left for me was to bow this old head of mine. Humbled by their way of life, I told myself that the important thing was to do your best, to consciously observe the commandments, and especially to be honest toward men and toward God. In respect of my new direction, my friends and comrades paused other problems. I could not force them to accompany me to a kosher restaurant if they felt differently. I have to admit that there was a cooling off in certain of the older relationships. It was a new way of living, to which one had to adapt progressively. I had found God, but I was not going to climb on top of roofs and yell, "I found God! Follow me!" My feelings about these matters are very personal, if not intimate, and awkward in trying to explain.

I have known many pious men who stopped observing and even stopped believing when they left the concentration camps where they had lost their families. They always ask me the same question: Where was God when they were murdering our wives and children? I had suffered in another way, by losing my mother and three brothers through extermination by the Lithuanians, and through all the years that have since gone by, I never stopped asking myself what hand and what compassionate power had protected my life. Was I better than my brothers? Of course not! I had no answer to this question, but it never left me in peace, and I continued to search for an answer with people who had more teaching and more knowledge of the Bible. I consulted people with university diplomas and religious erudition. They gave me different answers with which I was hardly satisfied and which even less satisfied my friends who continued to ask me where God had been. There were two people who gave me answers that at first glance seemed to be more in depth. The first was a doctor in his fifties, a pious man whom I found very agreeable to be around. From Deuteronomy 28 he sent me a text that deals with curses and blessings: "But if you do not listen to the voice of the eternal, your God; if you do not care to observe all his precepts and his laws that I am from this day commanding you, all of his curses will come upon you and against you and will overtake you; you will be damned in the city and damned in the fields, your sons and daughters will be given unto a foreign people and your eyes will look and will fail with longing for them all the day, and your hand will be impotent. The Lord will cause them to rise up against you until you are destroyed." The second response came from a Lubavitsher who explained the following to me. The Israelite people have been created as one unit, and each one is responsible for the whole community. The Torah is six hundred thousand words, as many words as there were Hebrews in biblical times. And if one letter becomes illegible, the Torah becomes unusable and the parchment must be rewritten. It is the same with people: if one person makes mistakes and does not observe God's laws, the people as a whole are responsible.

We children of murdered Jews are obviously unable to accept answers such as these. The Bible provides for the sentence of death for different mistakes that I will not enumerate here. In spite of everything, after the destruction of the Second Temple, we do not find a case where a death sentence was actually carried out, and we know that the rabbinic tribunals practiced justice while enveloping themselves with much circumspection and much clemency. Could it be that our God is any less forgiving? Rabbinic authorities must place themselves in the context of the times in which they live and must help survivors to finish their lives by offering answers that are both more humane and more realistic. For us, the survivors and our children, it is a very important problem because it raises the question of guilt. Are we, as survivors, guilty? Certain rabbis in Israel say so and directly incriminate the Ashkenazim and the culture to which we are heir. The answer is no, no, and no; we cannot accept this answer that opens the door to every bogus explanation.

Confronted by this same question from men who had lost their faith after the Shoah, the Israeli philosopher Yeshayahu Leibowitz answers without much gentleness: You never believed in God. You believed in God's help. It is in that belief that you have been disappointed. God did not help. But he who believes in God does not link his belief in the law to God's help. He believes in God because of his divinity and not because of the duties toward the human being that are attributed to him. As radical as this idea of faith may be, it probably corresponds to the ideal of a faith that would be truly selfless.

Another example of a lack of adaptation of the religion that I and a number of survivors hold dear is the institution of fasting. In the Jewish year, nine fasts are established. The two most important are the ninth of Av, when we commemorate the destruction of the two temples, and that of Yom Kippur. But sixty years after the Shoah, the rabbinate has not found a way to mark the greatest catastrophe suffered by the Jewish people. There is no fast commemorating the Shoah to pass down from one generation to another through the centuries. To appease the hearts of survivors is surely a mitzvah more important and more urgent than the numerous little rules whose meaning is mysterious. I always have hope that certain ears will be unplugged and certain eyes opened.

As I said in the preface, I write so that my grandchildren and the children of my grandchildren will have access to their own history in order that we don't forget what happened to our people. I know there are many books by survivors that have been written for the same reasons, and I consider it a sacred duty for all those who still can to give an account of our history and our destinies so that they will be transmitted to future generations. To not permit even a trace of all of these Jewish lives to be lost is, in my eyes, the greatest mitzvah, both a civic and a religious duty.

A Very Special Translation

The Invisible Jewish People of Lithuania

Isabelle Rozenbaumas,
translated by Jonathan Layton

Between 1994 and 1997 my father wrote his memoirs in Yiddish. The idea that I would translate them into French seemed natural to us, as it seemed to be self-evident that this task was incumbent upon me rather than any other translator. It was during an interruption of my first forward momentum that my father himself, tired of waiting, himself began a translation of his own book. In a French that was his and belonged to no one else.

The Yiddish manuscript had been written in black pencil, almost without any punctuation, which is to say in a language without the uppercase, with minimal indication of the beginning or end of sentences, in a rich and living language that was steadily refined in the process of the dive into writing. In its form, the French and Yiddish manuscripts had things in common, at least if you go by the school child's perforated sheets of paper, format 21/29 with large squares (or hand-drawn red lines), except it was now being written in pen. Nevertheless, here where the Yiddish flowed from the source, while sometimes borrowing from Russian technical, political, economic, or philosophic vocabulary or from internationalisms, my father's very rich French in the domains in which he was a heavily informed and astute reader was poetically fishing in the deep waters of the

Bescherelle[1] surrealist conjugations, inventing improbable syntaxes that stuck out like jetties in the infinite ocean of language and, above all, aiming high and low for idiomatic expressions, sometimes modeled on Yiddish, sometimes employing French in a perplexing way. But more than anything, my father discovered and adored words, French words. Nothing was more pleasing to him than to turn the dictionary around and discover two synonyms coveted with the same passion in one single sentence. An orgy of adverbs, of adjectives in apposition, of untranslated if not untranslatable puns, of asides to the incredulous reader, of transposed metaphors, of phrases appearing a little strange in French and remaining opaque as long as they had not mentally been retranslated into Yiddish. From this language that I call "the language of the father," *tate-loshn*, from his style modeled on the dialogued monologue of Yiddish, I made an effort to conserve the vivacity, the color, the taste, and hopefully more. Above all, in order to arrive at a perfectly natural style, I resisted the temptation to smooth out the language. I wanted the mark of thought in Yiddish to be seen and, if not the Yiddish accent in the French target language to be suggested, at least a perception of how we dealt with languages when we landed in France.

Thenceforth, it was no longer a question of translation, but of rewriting. And through the rewriting, the charge of betrayal hovered yet more menacingly. Unfortunately or perhaps, fortunately, this text resisted my comprehension more than the original Yiddish one to which I was unable to return because it had been lengthened in places, amended in others, shortened in still others. Faced with this narrative, with this story that I thought I knew by heart and that my father had now encrypted for me, his cooperation would be essential in the process of interpretation, without which the text would refuse to open. Every Thursday for a year and a half, Papa climbed the five flights to my apartment, sat down next to me with his manuscript in

1. *Le nouveau Bescherelle 1. L'art de conjuguer. Dictionnaire de 12000 verbes* (French ed.).

his hands, and performed the exegesis on his own text. We laughed a lot, and I cried a little. Being named Moishe (Moses), it was quite normal for him to write the Bible, he said slightly teasing me, in order for me to commentate on it. Religion was at the center of our arguments, where, good daughter, I took on the role of the nonbeliever. In a genuine dialogue between Jews, one of the two must assume this role.

In this atmosphere of the spoken and written word, I undertook the most far-flung voyage that it has been given me to make, the strangest, most exotic, a journey into the depths of my father's being. I hurried my step in the alleyways of his Telz shtetl, boisterous child, young rebel proletarian, lacking a father. I fled by his side along the roads and rivers of Asia. I rode horseback on the snow-covered trails of Russian forests. Ulysses, clearheaded and crafty, a hundred times I saw death in the face and came back to a ruined and submerged Ithaca.

During the same period of time I was making a film nurtured by this mentorship of my father, which had begun really with the first fragments of stories I had heard and now continued with our work of re-recreation, a film about Yiddish.[2] In returning to Lithuania, I was tying my story with his. My parents' accounts had long since imprinted on me the geography of Telz. Everywhere around me I was seeing the living world of the dead. In Telz, in the surrounding countryside, around our houses, our synagogues, our butcher shops, on the sites of mass murder, Jews constitute a mute and invisible people who continue to inhabit the places that they have filled for centuries with their activity and their fervor, with their discussions and their quarrels, a people of students without sidelocks and workers, polyglot teenage girls and observant women. My grandmother Mere-Khaye, who did not live long enough to become a grandmother, is among them. The massacre of men and boys from Telz where three

---

2. Isabelle Rozenbaumas and Michel Grosman, *Nemt: A Language without a People for a People without a Language* (2002; English version, 2004), a film about the resilience of Yiddish culture in Vilnius.

of her sons were shot took place in the first days of German occupation. She was murdered a few weeks later in the culmination of the innumerable torments Lithuanian collaborators of the Nazis inflicted on women and their youngest children.[3] She was around forty-five years old. She went through the ordeal of the women when they learned of the slaughter of the men and boys of Telz and was grieving her two youngest sons, Leybe and Elie. The one thing my father was ever able to utter about the massacre of his mother and her sufferings related to the horror and the shame such a decent human being must have felt when being forced to undress before being shot. The dignity of girls and women was destroyed before they were murdered.

We cannot be absolutely sure of what she knew of the fate of Yosef, her eldest. But of Moishe she knew he had been able to flee to the East, that he was resourceful, that he was intrepid, and that with God's help, he would live. This remarkable woman who spoke Lithuanian with her neighbors, read German, prayed in Hebrew, and lived in Yiddish left her imprint of tolerance and dignity, of profound and sincere humanism, on my father. Draped in her mystery, she never let anybody perceive her wound. Yet she had known everything of passion, sorrow, and affliction. From the very site where the torturers had penned the women and children from Telz before shooting them day after day, she has projected upon my life a light of love and hope.

Under the white stars of Lithuanian skies, I understood that Mere-Khaye had always walked with me, that she breathed in my breath, and that I had always been everywhere where she had been. My work of writing with my father, like my own endeavors, is an homage to her person, to her memory, and to her God about whom my father, myself, and our entire family have so much to say and to argue about.

---

3. I have described the Lithuanian distortions of the historical facts about their participation in the annihilation of the Jews in a text of 2000 written with Michel Grosman, published in the *Bulletin de l'Amicale d'Auschwitz* under the title "Les jeunes filles et la centrale nucléaire," partially reproduced on my website, http://batkamaat.org/?page_id=2212.

JONATHAN LAYTON, the translator, is a retired physician. He committed to this translation out of a fascination for the character of Moishe Rozenbaumas, a quintessential representation of Jewish heroism in the twentieth century. This book has represented a path between his Jewish American identity and the European history of his family.

ISABELLE ROZENBAUMAS, the editor, was trained as a historian. She has worked as a translator, editor, librarian (Musée d'Art et d'Histoire du Judaïsme, Paris), and filmmaker. A native Yiddish speaker, born in Vilna, she studied and taught Yiddish in different contexts, in Paris and New York. Her translations from English or Yiddish to French include Max Weinreich, Emanuel Ringelblum, Leib Rochman, Robert Alter, David Biale, Walter Laqueur, and Rabbi Jonathan Sachs. She wrote and directed with Michel Grosman the film *Nemt: A Language without a People for a People without a Language* about the resilience of Yiddish culture in Vilnius. She is the author of a research and artistic project about the education of the Jewish girls in interwar Lithuania in Gymnasium Yavne in Telz, developed on the website batkamaat.org. She worked with her father, Moishe Rozenbaumas, on the French version of his memoirs.